LEADING
SELF-ORGANISING
TEAMS

Workbook for Lean & Agile Professionals

Siegfried Kaltenecker

Leading Self-Organising Teams

Published by C4Media, publisher of InfoQ.com.

Production Editor: Ana Ciobotaru
Copyeditor: Professor Laurie Nyveen
Cover and Interior Design: Dragos Balasoiu

Library of Congress Cataloguing-in-Publication Data:
ISBN: 978-1-4303-2264-1
Printed in the United States of America

Prime Directive

"Regardless of what we discover, we understand and truly believe that everyone did the best job they could, given what they knew at the time, their skills and abilities, the resources available, and the situation at hand."

Norman L. Kerth (2001)

Contents

Why this workbook? 1

Self-organising teams...3
What are self-organising teams? 4
Why do we need self-organising teams? 11
What is leading self-organising teams all about?.................18

A model for leading self-organising teams.............27

Values of leading self-organising teams 33

Capabilities for leading self-organising teams........ 41
Focusing...42
Designing...61
Facilitating 85
Changing..100

Tools for focusing 125
Identify your customers and what they care about.............127
Team mission statement 128
Vision statement 130
Catch you if you can...131
Sharing perspectives on the team...132
Levels of team communication..133
Decision-making policies 135
Self-development 137
Managing the unexpected 138
Deciphering your company culture..140

Tools for designing 143
Micro-management assessment 145
Start with what you do now..147
Design your team charter..149
How to measure anything 150
Clarify where you start..152
Prerequisites for the design of a kanban system 155
Design your visual work-management system 157
Design your role as a manager...158

Design your action review cycle 159
Macro-management assessment 160

Tools for facilitating 163
Appreciative inquiry 165
Humble inquiry 167
Go-around 169
Chart writing 171
Standup meeting 173
Product review 175
Operations review 177
Retrospective facilitator's questionnaire 178
Large group events 179
World-café hosting guide 182
Open-space technology 184
Lean coffee 186

Tools for changing 189
Personal retrospective questionnaire 191
Exercises in looking into the future 193
Feedback and feed-forward 195
The feedback planner 196
Tricky situations: Worksheet for preparation 197
Guidelines for setting up a change team 198
Stakeholder mapping 199
Guidelines for stakeholder interviews 202
Visual change-management systems 204
Change canvases 206
References 207
About the author and acknowledgments 212

Why this workbook?

"The best architectures, requirements, and designs emerge from self-organising teams," the Agile Manifesto announces. This raises a few questions. What are self-organising teams? Why do we need them? What difference do self-organising teams make? How can we support self-organisation?

This book provides practice-based answers to these questions. Focused on helping lean and agile professionals to improve, these answers want to encourage:

- a clear understanding of what self-organisation is about and why we need it to meet the challenges of the 21st century,
- a profound overview on what is needed to successfully lead in a self-organising environment, and
- the willingness to enhance your own capabilities by continuously practicing and making good use of the broad collection of proven tools I offer.

In 2005, when I got to know Scrum, I was immediately intrigued by its emphasis on collaboration across multiple boundaries. I had seen lean management and XP practices before but hadn't been fully aware of their impact on teamwork and customer feedback. In the following years, while working with many teams as well as managers on "becoming agile", I felt more and more confused about what agility actually means. In 2010, discovering kanban for IT, systemic self-organisation was atop my menu again.

Kanban's fourth principle seems to summarise the main theme of this workbook: encourage leadership at all levels. In this regard, I have written the book to show how this can be done. Whether you are a senior developer or a team lead, ScrumMaster or junior tester, head of engineering or product manager everybody is needed to effectively lead your team, everybody contributes to the overall success of your enterprise, and everybody shares management responsibility. In short, everybody is part of what I call "leadership as a team sport".

By combining fundamentals (the "why"), specific values and capabilities (the "what"), and practical tools (the "how"), this book tries to be as much of a cookbook as possible. Its recipes use mainly three ingredients: first, the essence of what I learned from reading, combining resources from various disciplines, even trying to bridge gaps between US and European thinking; second, the distillate of my most important insights from discussions with friends and colleagues; third, the spice given by multiple clients I have worked with.

I cannot but hope this book helps to improve your cooking efforts – or at best, that it inspires you to create your own recipes and develop your capabilities in the specific kitchen around you. Since my own gourmet journey isn't over either, I'd be happy to get feedback from your experiences.

Sigi Kaltenecker
Vienna, December 2014

PART
ONE

Self-organising teams

What are self-organising teams?

"Knowledge workers have to manage themselves. They have to have autonomy," leadership guru Peter Drucker states in his *Management Challenges for the 21st Century* (Drucker 1999, p.123). This resonates with the agile idea that "self-organising teams choose how best to accomplish their work, rather than being directed by others outside the team" (Schwaber and Sutherland 2013). But what are self-organising teams? What is self-organisation about? What qualifies a group of individuals to be a team?

Let's start with the last question. **What are teams?** In line with team expert J. Richard Hackman (Hackman 2002), I see that this is often far from clear. The term "team" works a bit like a Rorschach test: people read into it what they wish. They have different things in mind when they think and talk of teams. In many cases, real teams get confused with so-called co-acting groups. Whereas co-acting groups consist of people working in proximity to one another but not dependent on what the others do to complete their respective jobs, **real teams have four features:**

- joint tasks to fulfil a compelling mission;
- clear boundaries in terms of information flow, alignment with other organisational units, resources, and decision-making policies;
- authority to self-manage within these boundaries; and
- stability over some reasonable period of time.

In deciding the extent of a team's authority, one must mindfully consider who is in the best position to handle each of four functions that must be fulfilled:

- setting directions for the team, i.e. specifying the organisational objectives, the core purpose or mission that spawns the myriad of smaller tasks;
- designing the performing unit and arranging for needed organisational support for the work, i.e. structuring tasks, deciding who will be involved in performing them, establishing norms of conduct for work behaviour, and making sure team members have the resources and assistance they need to carry out their work;

- monitoring and managing the work process, i.e. collecting and interpreting data about how the work is proceeding and initiating corrective action as needed;
- executing the work, i.e. applying physical or mental energy to accomplish tasks.

By allotting these core functions to the responsibility areas of either management or team, Hackman provides us with an authority matrix to distinguish four levels of team self-organisation (figure 1).

Since the world is not only black and white, I see more than one form of self-organisation. To me, self-organisation is rather an umbrella term for a continuum that encompasses:

- **manager-led teams** that leave team members only the authority for task execution while managers monitor and manage work processes, design the context, and set the direction. From our point of view, many expert groups in functional silos as well as traditional project-management "teams" are practical examples of this setup;
- **self-managing teams** that put members in charge of executing tasks and for managing their progress (within IT, we see a lot of kanban teams applying this approach, either focusing on team tasks or on team-bridging value streams);
- **self-designing teams** that give members the authority to modify the design of their team and/or aspects of the organisational context in which they operate (most real management teams are in this position as are some Scrum teams – especially when lean/agile is scaled);
- **self-governing teams** that have responsibility for all four core functions as shown by corporate boards of directors, worker cooperatives, or startups.

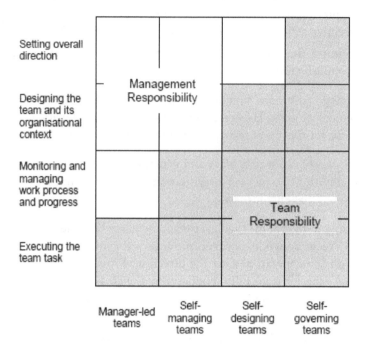

Figure 1: Hackman's authority matrix.

Laws of self-organisation

Despite all these structural differences, all kinds of self-organising teams share a few characteristics. According to Francis Heylighen, author of "The science of self-organization and adaptivity" (2001), all self-organising systems are characterised by:

- distributed control, i.e. absence of centralised control;
- continuous adaptation to a changing environment;
- emergent structure from local interaction;
- feedback, both positive and negative; and
- resilience due to the system's ability to repair and adjust.

Referring to the original "principle of the self-organising dynamic system" as formulated by the cybernetician Ross Ashby in 1947, Heylighen helps us to understand that self-organisation is kind of the natural process by which global order arises out of the local interactions between the components of an initially disordered system. Thus, self-organisation is the rule, not the exception, in systemic behaviour. Even in the agile world, it is neither "a breath of fresh air" (Schwaber 2001) nor "a secret sauce" (Sutherland 2008).

Despite all the fashionable metaphors we use, self-organisation is a law that is applicable to many different systems. There is a broad variety of examples from neuroscience, physics, chemistry, and biology: the brain with all its connected neurons that construct mental models without relying on central control; plants such as aspen groves, the largest known living organisms on Earth with each tree connected to all others by a single underground root system; flocks of birds, herds of elk, or flocks of sheep moving in a synchronised manner as if they were a single animal to avoid danger or change course; or ants creating a system of finding food out of seemingly random movements.

What conclusions can we draw from these insights? What do the laws of systemic behaviour mean for self-organising teams in a business environment? First of all, we should remind ourselves that self-organising teams do not happen overnight. Nor is self-organisation something that happens once and remains forever within its initial boundaries. As a matter of fact, a team is never done with the process of self-organisation. The members have to continually reorganise themselves in a sense-and-respond manner to shifting demands and contexts. In other words, self-organisation is an on-going process: whenever the setup changes, the organisation and the team need to repeat the whole process.

Self-organisation is not just about the whole team within its specific organisational context. **Each team member has to self-organise as well** to figure out what to do and how to do it. And every day, every member has to coordinate his or her self-organisation with the rest of the team. In order to synchronise, we run regular meetings such as the daily stand-ups, operations reviews, and retrospectives.

Another pillar of all self-organising teams is the **tricky balance of similarity and difference**. Paradoxically, in order to effectively exploit their differences, team members need to share enough similarities. As German systems thinker Diether Gebert shows in his data-driven survey on innovative teams (2004), team members must trust each other in the first place. Without a certain amount of trust in advance, they can neither explore their individual backgrounds nor inspect and adapt current work processes. Later on, an appropriate balance of recognition and reward as well as fair play is important for further self-empowerment. Disrespect kills self-organisation in a similar way to social loafing.

It is a truism that self-organising teams need effective interaction to realise their full potential. What Russell Ackoff says about systems in general (Ackoff 1994) holds true for a team: its performance **is not the sum of its parts but the product of their interaction.** However, self-organisation does not mean the team members get to decide everything themselves. Self-organising teams are not boundary-less. On the contrary, a clear set of expectations and responsibilities is needed to contain self-organisation.

The C/D/E model

In her landmark dissertation, *Conditions for Self-Organizing in Human Systems* (2002), Glenda Eoyang points out three conditions that must be met for the self-organising process to generate coherent patterns:

- **A containing (C) boundary** surrounds the system to define its identity. Simply speaking, there is no clear "self" without a clear separation of "the other ones". This kind of container builds on organisational pillars such as a clear-cut mission, a compelling direction and challenging goals, operating guidelines, and clear decision-making policies.

- **There are significant differences (D)** in knowledge, experience, education, age, gender, or cultural background. High performing teams know how to acknowledge and incorporate the diversity of the team and how to build on the differences that make a difference.
- **Transforming exchange (E)** guides the interactions both within the team and with its environment. This transfer of information, energy or material between interdependent people or units is critical to the ability to self-organise into system-wide patterns.

Far from being a pure constraint, a boundary always marks an opportunity for communication. As such, a boundary has effects in both directions. In Margaret Wheatley's words (2006), "if people are free to make their own decisions, guided by a clear organisational identity for them to reference, the whole system develops greater coherence and strength. The organisation is less controlling but more orderly."

As part of a bigger system, each unit of the C/D/E model is dependent on a supportive context. In J. Richard Hackman's metaphor (2002) , "if a well-designed work team is a seedling, then the organisational context is the soil in which it is planted, the milieu that provides the nutrients needed for it to grow and bear fruit." Less metaphorically speaking, Hackman gauges that the contextual support for self-organising teams consists basically of four subsystems:

- information, in terms of providing teams the data that members need to competently plan and execute their work;
- infrastructure, in terms of appropriate physical space (a factor many co-located teams struggle with), technical infrastructure, and money;
- education, in terms of any training, coaching, or technical assistance the team may need; and
- reward, in terms of providing positive economic as well as symbolic consequences for good team performance.

Coming back to Eoyang's model of self-organisation, we can now draw a simple picture that shows how container, difference, exchange, and context play together.

Figure 2 contains elements of different size, shape, and colour in its centre, representing team member's differences in background, strengths, and skill sets. As the linking arrows show, members are connected to each other, building up a cross-functional team by intense exchanges. The whole team interaction is surrounded by a containing boundary, partly dotted to indicate that this container is an open rather than a closed system. Far from being a classical black box for its environment, the team is in constant exchange with its environment.

The team also needs a supportive context in terms of the indicated subsystems of infrastructure, information, education, and reward. And they need an external agent, represented by the yellow-white-orange circle, who is responsible for containment as well as support. This is the role of the line manager. I will come back to this role and the role-play between manager and self-organising team in the chapter on designing.

Although eliminated from the picture to keep it as simple as possible, the interdependence of the team, its connectedness in terms of the whole value stream, and the necessary organisational awareness are key to any self-organising process.

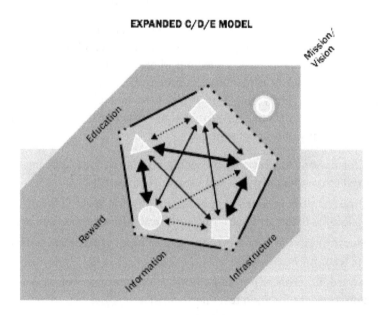

Figure 2: Expanded C/D/E model.

Why do we need self-organising teams?

From the 1980s onward, we experienced a tremendous amount of change:

- political changes, such as the end of the Soviet Union and the bloc of Eastern European countries;
- societal changes such as intensified migration and increased education in many countries;
- demographic changes, with higher life expectancy and decreasing birth rates in the Western hemisphere;
- ecological changes such as global warming and climate change;
- technological changes, e.g. in medicine, biology, and in communication technology, giving birth to a generation of "digital natives"; and
- economic changes, from the tyranny of shareholder value and the rise of the so-called BRICS countries to the global financial crises in 2008.

All these changes brought with them new demands. Organisations have no longer been able to choose whether they want to respond to these demands or not. Change has become mandatory. Trying to hold on to the status quo is like trying to keep the leaves on trees in autumn. For an organisation to be successful, it must adequately deal with the risks and use the opportunities every change brings. In other words, the organisation must keep up with or, ideally, be ever so slightly ahead of current market demands. How inconvenient then that this market behaves unpredictably? That which is on top today can be a flop tomorrow; yesterday's success factor can become a burden overnight.

Business agility turns out to be the new mantra for the successful running of an organisation in the 21st century. Improvement and innovation have long since become mandatory for any organisation. Available opportunities should be used, new possibilities discovered, competitive edges honed.

Self-organising teams seem to be kind of a miracle solution to many of these problems. They are said to:

- achieve better results;

- deliver more business value;
- collaborate more effectively than micro-managed teams;
- learn faster;
- work with more motivation and fun; and
- be more rewarding.

Managers who are busy projecting their wishes onto self-organising teams are displaying a crucial blind spot: self-organisation is as much about the management as it is about the team. The need for more agility is also nurtured by the fact that traditional command-and-control management turned out to be dysfunctional. Stifling bureaucracy, suffocating control systems, and the empty rituals of planning and performance management are just a few symptoms of this dysfunction.

According to the 2013 Shift Index from Deloitte's Center for the Edge, only one in five employees is fully engaged, 75% of employees lack motivation and passion, and only 15% of all teams are able to realise their full potential. There is also a growing amount of change fatigue due to the fact that many change initiatives do not achieve the intended goals. Teams meet these initiatives with an attitude of "not again!" rather than commitment. There are no comprehensive figures but various sample surveys indicate that between 60% and 80% of projects end in failure.

There is a **variety of reasons for this depressing failure rate**: lack of transparency; too many change initiatives in parallel; weak change agency; missing feedback loops; and, last but not least, obsession with detailed project plans, predesigned milestones, and the prediction of clear-cut outcomes. Unfortunately, all the turbulence around us makes a mockery of our plans and predictions. As Meg Wheatley writes (1999, p. 87), "It's time to realise that we will never cope with this new world using our old maps."

Let's examine a table that depicts the organisational paradigm common in the last century with a modern perspective to better understand what the necessary change is about.

20th Century	21st Century
Organisations as centralised functions and silos	Organisations as whole systems
Predictable cause-and-effect relationships	Complex networks and webs of relationships

Central coordination and control required	Decentralized processes of self-organisation and self-regulation
Hierarchy and bureaucracy	Lean networks
Primarily oriented towards shareholder value	Balanced orientation around all stakeholders
Administration orients towards short-term profit	Orientation towards long-term success through improvement and innovation
Employees as functional experts following instructions	Employees as cross-functional team workers using their joint expertise
Change is project-driven and reactive	Change is seen as continuous and adaptive

Table 1: Paradigms of organisations.

The table summarises some of the key differences between **mechanistic and systemic thinking** as outlined by Russell Ackoff more than 20 years ago (Ackoff 1994). Even though the table tends to polarise a bit too much, it outlines the systemic context of past and future-oriented leadership. The dominant organisational paradigms resonate with the basic values and principles of two very different models of how to manage and lead: functional versus holistic setup; linear cause and effect versus complexity thinking; administration versus continuous innovation; shareholder value versus interests of all stakeholders; change as an exception versus change as key driver of any business.

We should not forget that self-organising teams are not just a matter of efficacy. Today, many knowledge workers demand a high degree of autonomy. They want to make the most of their expertise rather than follow instructions and to work in teams rather than alone. They want to do something that makes sense to them, to have fun at work, and to see how their achievements contribute to the companýs overall success. Last but not least, they request working conditions that help them to develop their capabilities.

Thus, the former administrator of standardised business processes is supposed to become an organisational designer for high-performing teams. The abilities to set clear goals, establish modes of decision-making, and free up resources are also a part of this. The trouble is that the principles and values of the mechanistic paradigm are still pretty much in place. They still guide old-school management practices in many organisations—and, perhaps even worse, the educational concepts at universities. Despite all the new challenges around us, the traditional MBA is still seen as key qualification for a manager.

From business agility to agile management

But is business administration really what is needed to deal with the current challenges? As Jeremy Hope and Robin Fraser, founders of the highly influential Beyond Budgeting Round Table, put it (Hope and Fraser 2003, p.29), "For most organizations today, their success factors have changed and their strategy is changing, but their management processes, leadership styles, and cultures are lagging behind."

Figure 3: Side effects of change.

This raises the question of what a future-oriented leadership model can look like. What is needed to meet the current challenges? Why do we think that effectively leading self-organising teams is key to succeed in the 21st century? What values, skills, and techniques are needed to support rather than hinder self-organisation? Over the course of the last decade, we answered a lot of these questions. From a variety of modern literature as well as from my own consulting experience, I observe some recurring themes:

- Old-fashioned command and control gives way to a modern culture that respects self-control without losing sight of the organisation-wide need for coordination.

- New forms of network-oriented leadership appear alongside hierarchical management in order to use the available expertise optimally, last but not least in response to environmental dynamics.

- If managers still try to control both people and activity, constricting team members' freedom and inhibiting local change, they only create conditions that threaten the organisation's survival.

- To focus on self-control is the only way to show respect and effectively exploit and capitalise on the capabilities of well-trained knowledge workers.

- Encouraging decentralised decision making while keeping an overview by applying visual management, and establishing fast feedback loops and selected team-performance metrics is a sure path to better alignment and intrinsic motivation of teams.

- As figure 4 suggests, the traditional role of a superior captain who directs functional experts in a centralised way gives way to decentralised, network-oriented **"leadership as a team sport"**. This team sport relies on clear boundaries, mutual relationships, and fast feedback loops between all team members.

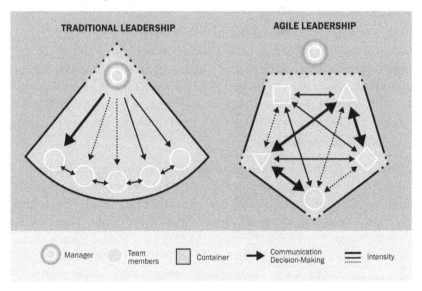

Figure 4: Traditional versus agile leadership.

Far from being purely theoretical, our old maps are kind of the source code for dysfunctional behaviour – and the root cause of numerous organisational problems. On the one hand, these maps create a high degree of demotivation. There is an increasing amount of turnover and burnout, often leading to the loss of key players who are tired of fighting windmills. This results in an obvious gap between what companies must achieve and what people want to invest. No wonder that the average life expectancy of organisations is less than 20 years. On the other hand, managers are forced to acknowledge a fundamental paradox: that they are individually responsible for the behaviour of a complex social system they cannot control. Amidst a turbulent environment, management inevitably has to deal with an often-overwhelming amount of uncertainty, unpredictability, and risk.

Given the present complexity, no single person is able to capture let alone process it appropriately. Mental overload is inevitable. At best, a manager can build on probabilities; at worst, a manager's actions and decisions are purely random. No "management by" method offers an escape from this fate, whether it pretends to be scientific or not. Managers have to accept the difficulty of controlling social systems. Rather than superior directors of their organisations, managers are more the proverbial fly riding on the trunk of an elephant. The fly is convinced that it is steering the elephant, the elephant does not mind, and it all makes the ride more interesting.

Both external and internal factors underscore the need to change how we run our organisations. **In order to become more agile, we must transfer more power and authority to people closer to the customer**. We have to trust them with information and give them time to think, learn, and improve. At the same time, structural costs must be slashed and bureaucracy reduced if not eliminated. "Lean" is the right keyword for this effort.

The only way to achieve these goals is to empower our teams. We have to allow them to use the full measure of their expertise, not only in executing their work but also in monitoring and controlling themselves, making their own decisions, and even designing their processes. This may be seen as a question of natural respect. As I stated at the beginning of this chapter, knowledge workers such as IT experts have to have autonomy. My experience shows that capitalising on autonomy is both a question of team training and organisational change. Again, self-organisation does not happen overnight. Since the containers for this self-organisation are still restricted in various ways, let alone chronically disturbed by micro-management and lacking work design, to capitalise on self-organising processes needs fundamental changes. If **effective empowerment is an equation of freedom multiplied by capability**, we need to learn new things and unlearn old patterns.

This equation reminds us that self-organising is not a technical process. Although we have to deal with a lot of structural issues, there are always emotions involved: positive ones such as pride, excitement, and fun, but also negative emotions such as confusion, uncertainty, and fear. Both categories of emotion are two sides of the same coin and are typical phenomena in change processes.

From this point of view, it comes as no surprise that in most cases, both management and team feel a measure of ambivalence when about to transfer authority. As always, when we question the foundation of a person's self-esteem (e.g. roles, responsibilities, resources), some individuals may feel overwhelmed while others are puzzled. As German change-management pioneers Doppler and Lauterburg (2000) show, there are three basic questions about impending change that immediately pop up:

- **Do I need to do this?** Do I understand why we need self-organising teams? Are these teams mandatory or are there alternatives? What do we expect of self-organisation?
- **Can I do this?** Am I able to deal with what self-organising will mean to us? Do I have all the skills I need to become self-organising? What are my chances for good results? What counts as success under the new conditions?
- **Do I want it?** Is self-organisation interesting? What's in it for me? Is there any risk of loss of money, relationships, or career prospects? Can I expect to gain something from the change?

"We're all for improvement but why do we have to change?" asked a member of an operations team, pointing out the ambivalence many feel towards self-organisation processes. These processes cannot be simply imposed. Professional change management is needed from the very beginning with:

- profound information (why self-organise?);
- clear expectations (how to measure success?);
- state-of-the-art facilitation (how to guide the transformation?); and

- continuous training and coaching (what do you need to know and do?).

What is leading self-organising teams all about?

//

What exactly do we have to do to capitalise on self-organisation? How can we best support our teams? What special kind of leadership is needed?

Returning to my idea of "leadership as a team sport", let me use the analogy of a soccer team to better describe what this might be about. What can we learn from soccer for leading in a dynamic environment? Perhaps the most important lesson is to succeed as a team, i.e. to win a game based on the willingness and ability of players to help each other. This help builds on many skills:

- **the skill** to professionally understand and master a specific role on the team (goalkeeper, defender, midfielder, striker) and how this role is supposed to interact with the other roles;
- **physical skills** such as running, blocking or tackling your opponent, jumping, heading, or bending;
- **technical ball skills** such as properly passing and receiving, dribbling, tricking, holding, and kicking;
- **tactical skills** such as understanding the concept of the game as well as the flow of certain moves and play without the ball, such as when each player has to decide whether to be part of an attack or stay

behind to secure the defence, running to be in the right place at the right time, running to draw the attention of an opponent away from other players, and the like; and

- **strategic skills** that allow a player to view of the situation on the field and act accordingly, to be aware of opportunities to attack and score, to exploit the routines of standard situations (e.g. free kicks or corners), and to respond to changing game situations as quickly as possible.

Certainly, the contribution of each player in terms of passes completed and tactical importance is always different. Network analysis (see figure 5) shows that there are always players who are more active than others (activity is shown by size of circle). But this does not necessarily mean that the most active players dominate the whole game. Part of the fascination of team sports is that anybody can score the decisive goal - even the goalkeeper, as we know from some of the most spectacular moments of soccer history.

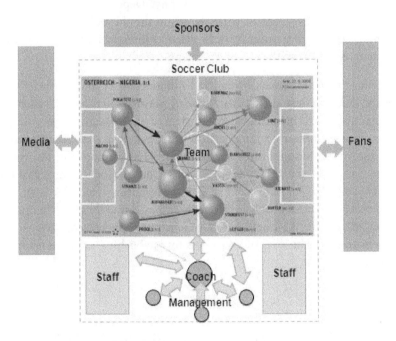

Figure 5: The soccer system.

What is the role of the coach? To control the game? To steer the team? Does the coach monitor every move? Is the coach involved at all? Actually, a coach's influence on the game's progress is limited. Once a match has started, a soccer team is a self-organising unit that follows a specific dynamic. Regardless of whether a coach presents himself or herself as one of the stars, jumps around in the coaching zone, shouts instructions to key players, or insults the referee, there is no opportunity to control what is going on in the field. The team is on its own to perform the best they can.

Does this mean that a coach is superfluous? Definitely not. From a systemic point of view, the coach greatly influences the team's composition, tactics, training program, playing style, and so on. The coach is the one who focuses the team and sets its boundaries. Together with the managing director and other leaders, the coach decides who plays, buys or sells players, runs academies for young players, scouts for talent, and the like. Together with the club staff, from marketing to maintenance, the coach nurtures a particular club culture, establishes a certain reputation, and contributes to the business, and so on. Last but not least, the coach influences the team's interaction by his or her understanding of soccer, often referred to as the game philosophy. Depending on the coach's underlying assumptions of what the game should look like in order to win, the team will train, play, and review its internal interactions as well as its interactions with various opponents.

During the game, the coach can still influence the team´s interactions. He or she can create novelty by replacing players, communicate with the captain, or use the break between the halves to change tactics. Interestingly, even though there are a lot of options, the main task of the soccer coach is observation, systems thinker Fritz Simon (2004) points out. The coach observes each individual player as well as the specific exchanges of the whole team and their interaction with the opposing team. Furthermore, the coach provides professional feedback based on the observations. In line with Simon, we might say that the primary purpose of the coach is to create the right level of awareness by establishing accurate feedback loops.

Self-organising soccer systems

This is far from being airy-fairy stuff. The feedback loops between the team and the coach heavily affect how social structures are built. They drive the process of collective sense making. While banned from the field of play during the game, the coach is a classic boundary keeper, with important influence on the game's dynamic without the opportunity to directly intervene.

Figure 5 reminds us that the dynamic of a soccer game is also strongly influenced by the broader organisational context of the soccer system. The soccer system is not limited to team interactions. On the contrary, it is co-created by external stakeholders like fans, the media, and the sponsors who spend a lot of money to see their team win.

The notorious 12th-man phenomenon, when hometown fans use excitement for their team to create an energetic advantage, reminds us that fans are also a self-organising system. The same holds the other way round, when outraged fans, seeing their team lose for the fifth time in a row, boo and whistle, curse players, and even force players into direct conversation after the game (sometimes, at the edge of the field, literally bridging the gap between the soccer system and its stakeholders). Think of media criticising individual players or the team, demoralising them and putting them under pressure. Or think of the enormous influence owners and sponsors may have on the design of the soccer system by hiring or firing coaches, purchasing players, and recomposing the whole team. All interactions between these specific systems potentially change the container, introduce differences, and thereby create new forms of exchange.

What parallels do we see between soccer and self-organised teams? What conclusions can we draw for leadership in an agile business environment?

In order to set appropriate boundaries for answering these questions, let's start with some obvious limitations of the analogy:

- Soccer is for sure an oversimplification of real business dynamics, which are limited neither to a field that allows everybody to observe and keep track of what is going on nor to a simple matter of playing against one clearly identifiable opponent. The need to quickly respond to unpredictable changes in a business environment is nurtured by far more complex factors.

- In business, there is no such thing as a clearly marked field with stable boundaries and a constant set of rules. On the contrary, change is one of the key challenges to a business. Daily business is more like playing many games in parallel, not always with reasonable rules and sometimes even dependent on each other.

- In contrast to soccer or other team sports, boundaries and constraints change a lot. Think of new regulations (e.g. financial or political ones), strategic impediments (saturated markets in general, aggressive competitors in particular), or new games emerging without a clear set of rules that force experienced experts to act more like amateurs than professionals.

- Soccer players are usually not knowledge workers, although it is said that it needs a certain amount of intelligence to win a game.

If we are willing to accept these limitations, the soccer analogy still gives us food for thought.

First of all, neither team sports nor enterprises are predictable. You don't know the results in advance and you have no idea what the game will look like. Even if a team has won six games in a row, there is no guarantee that it will win the seventh. And even the most successful product or service strategy that has paid off for several years can fail in the future. As we know from airline safety instructions, "turbulence can occur unexpectedly."

Second, soccer, like business, is basically value-driven. What do you value most, when the time comes to compose a new team? What are your guiding principles? What policies do you prefer?

Third, the power of a team is directly correlated to the flow of communication and decision making: where to run to, where to pass the ball, when to attack a member of the opposing team, when to strike, and the like. Intra-team interaction is defined by the differences between team members and by players' varying amounts of activity. Significantly, the most active players are not necessarily the ones who make or break the game. Both in soccer and in business, success is the product of the whole team's interaction within their specific network.

Fourth, in both team sports and business, awareness is very important. Effective leadership is directly correlated with the ability to set a joint focus and establish a certain culture of feedback. If a team does not agree on where to pay attention, decision making is hard if not impossible. In such cases, the team's actions may remind us of Monty Python's famous "100 yards for people with no sense of direction".

In soccer, as in business, there is usually no way of staying in line with an initial plan. For sure, in most cases there is a specific constellation of players (i.e. the composition of your team), some tactic for the specific game (i.e. how to achieve the goal), and the overall objective of winning something big (i.e. kind of a release plan). But from the first minute on, each team member has to react to what is really going on rather than stick to the initial plan. The team has to identify unexpected challenges (i.e. impediments) and quickly respond to changing situations (i.e. new demands, negative feedback from the customer, and the like). In short, the whole team has to establish its own feedback loops to inspect and adapt as needed.

Shared leadership

This resonates with the current debate about leadership as an amorphous phenomenon that has to be examined for its relational aspects. Nowadays, few if any theorists ignore the complexity of relationships that contributes to a team's – let alone the whole organisation's – effectiveness.

We can begin to see that team leadership is not something that resides in a few experts, regardless of their status as specialists, key players, or formal managers. Instead, it is a system-wide capacity directly related to how open the organisation is to new, especially disconfirming information and how effectively that information can be processed by anyone in the organisation. Even more, systems thinkers state that leadership is best thought of as a behaviour, not a role. We need acts of leadership in various situations, but various people can satisfy these needs. Hence, we have to focus on leadership as it is practiced in daily interactions. Our business is driven by the process-driven character of leading, the "social flow of interacting and connecting" (Crevani, Lindgren, and Packendorf 2010, p.79) rather than by general definitions and static management roles. The process of leading cannot be centred on individual managers with extraordinary personality traits such as charisma, authenticity, and natural authority. Given the complex challenges of the 21st century, the responsibilities, competencies, and decision making need to be distributed amongst several individuals – and self-organising teams are a catalyst for this sort of distribution.

In the context of the modern organisation, team-based leadership has far-reaching consequences. It demonstrates that the success of an organisation is the result of the collaboration of highly varied forces. The effectiveness of these forces does not depend on the formal position ("I am the manager a.k.a. playmaker"). Rather, effectiveness ("winning games, with regard to the final victory of the cup") depends on the relevant capabilities in the specific situation at hand ("in this game situation, I am leading our attack").

The conceptual shift from leadership captured in one role that is the property of an individual (the manager) to leadership as a trait of the system goes hand in hand with the shift from managing work to managing flow. Management methods such as Scrum, Lean, or Kanban explicitly encourage everybody in the system to do more than just business as usual – whether it is on the level of team, department, project, matrix organisation, or business unit. Besides managing their own work, members must pay attention to how work is coordinated in order to create value for the customer. Leadership as a team sport, then, means motivating each member to manage the system and bring in specific impulses for further improvement.

Again, this team-based approach to leadership resonates with the reports from Agile practitioners interviewed for our *Successful Leadership in an Agile World* study (Kaltenecker et al. 2011). Across multiple companies, backgrounds, and expertise, the hierarchy-bridging and cross-functional collaboration of different experts has been a decisive factor for extraordinary results. Leadership emerged from various sources and was not limited to formal management positions.

The practical experience resonates with theoretical discussions of **leadership as a trait of the system rather than that of an individual manager**. With the publication of Katzenbach and Smith's classic *The Wisdom of Teams* (1993), shared leadership became a part of the lexicon.

Shared leadership means that all team members:

- take on responsibility for the overall success just as much as for individual development;
- achieve and "sell" results together;
- situationally distribute authority in favour of technical as well as social competence;
- establish network-like communication models;
- bring decisions approved by all colleagues to the centre of actions;
- force critical examination of work processes and, if necessary, adaptation; and
- subject the quality of collaboration to regular consideration.

With his model of a "leaderful practice", Joseph Raelin (2003) goes a step further. He defines four qualities of contemporary leadership. In Raelin's view, leadership is **concurrent** in terms of the simultaneous acts of leadership, **collective** in terms of a shared responsibility that cannot be delegated to hierarchical superiors, **collaborative** in terms of intensive teamwork, and **compassionate** as each team member supports the others. Later on, we will see how these features resonate with the core capabilities of leading self-organising teams.

PART
TWO

A model for leading
self-organising teams

What does the soccer analogy mean for modern organisations? What values can we build on? What specific capabilities do we need to encourage leadership at all levels? What tools can help us master business agility?

I would like to present a model for leading self-organising teams that tries to answer these questions. This model is the current summary of both my research and my practical experience in training, facilitating, and coaching. I am fully aware that this model does not represent the end of the road (if there is one). Certainly, it is an oversimplification of what is really needed to successfully lead your lean and agile business. As the old saying goes, all models are wrong although some are useful.

With all due respect to my own limitations, I know that this model has proven to be useful in many situations. It helped customers to better understand what they are doing (or should be doing), it encouraged various experiments in shared leadership, it ignited intense conversations with peers, and, last but not least, it provided kind of a map with which to orient myself in unknown territories.

An expedition into uncertainty

In his book Sensemaking in Organizations, American organizational scientist Karl Weick tells the story of a Hungarian military unit carrying out a maneuver in the Swiss Alps (Weick 1985). Surprised by a storm, this unit went missing for two days in the snow and ice, and all hope of recovery seemed lost. However, three days later, the soldiers returned, uninjured, to their base camp.

How did the unit manage to extricate itself from this hopeless situation? The unit commander explained that after they had given up hope, one of the soldiers found a map in his rucksack. Everyone instantly relaxed, struck camp, and survived the snowstorm. The next day, the commander led his troops back to base camp with the help of the map.

It was quite a surprise when they later discovered that the map showed not the Swiss Alps but the Pyrenees.

Basically, the model consists of **values, capabilities, and tools**. Figure 6 displays these areas for leading self-organising teams in the form of the steering wheel of a ship.

The hub contains four values: respect, commitment, simplicity, and courage. These values from the lean and agile world resonate the most with me. As you will find out, my understanding is highly influenced by what has already been said in Lean, XP, Scrum, and Kanban. I have reframed these values partly to better refer to my experience. In general, our value system guides the way we make sense of the world. That's why I put these values at the centre of the steering wheel; they comprise the hub of all your leadership activities.

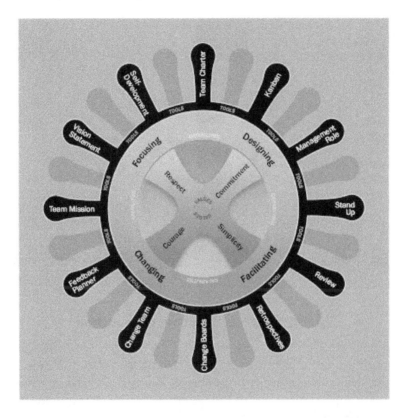

Figure 6: A simple model for leading self-organising teams.

The middle area focuses on the four capabilities I see as crucial for effectively leading self-organising teams: focusing, designing, facilitating, and changing. Just like the values, these capabilities are not mutually exclusive. On the contrary, they represent signposts rather than absolute cornerstones of what is needed. As figure 6 suggests, some of these signposts point in a similar direction, others point in very different directions. Less metaphorically speaking, several features of focusing such as value orientation or waste reduction heavily overlap with designing skills such as visual work management or flow management. On the other hand, design needs facilitating to take place in any organisational context. For instance, you will not establish a system for fast feedback loops without the ability to observe, listen, and guide the interactions of your team. But facilitating also means designing the right conditions for people to effectively interact. Finally, changing requires both designing and facilitating to set the focus on regular inspection and adaption, let alone on a system to create a sustainable change flow.

Figure 7: Signposts at the Cape of Good Hope.

The outer area represents the tools that let you practise your value-driven capabilities. Although the figure identifies just a few examples, the blank handles in grey suggest that you can use multiple tools to achieve a certain impact. Referring to the idea of leadership as a team sport, the high number of handles emphasises at least four things:

1. You need more than one capability.

2. Teams use more than one tool to successfully meet their business challenges.

3. The wheel is not steered by one but many captains. As long as a single joint mission drives these captains, teamwork is welcome in effectively steering the course.

4. All these potential captains will use different handles to steer their ship in different weather.

In the following chapters, I will dive deeper into each area to provide a better introduction into the values, more insight into each core capability, and a broad variety of tools that were helpful to many of my clients.

Since there's a good chance are good to end up as the proverbial fool with a tool, I will also try to highlight the necessary attitude both teams and managers need to successfully lead self-organising systems.

PART
THREE

Values of leading
self-organising teams

"What matters now?" management guru Gary Hamel asks in one of his latest books (Hamel 2012). "Values" is his first answer. Why do values matter? They matter because they guide the ways we make sense of the world. Although often used in an inflationary way, values such us respect, openness, and commitment are far more than just rhetoric. On the contrary, values both guide our individual actions and nurture our corporate culture.

From an organisational point of view, values can be seen as part of the core purpose of a business. Whereas the mission defines the hard core of this purpose (what is our reason for existence?), values are the soft factors that make or break this mission.

From a personal point of view, values are best defined as what is truly important to me. It is what I really care about, what I appreciate and literally build on. In the lean/agile world, values play a prominent role. They set new boundaries for behaviour and decision-making in the technology business, for instance: communication, simplicity, feedback, and courage for XP; commitment, focus, openness, respect, and courage for Scrum; transparency, balance, collaboration, customer focus, flow, leadership, understanding, agreement, and respect for kanban.

The reason why I chose commitment, simplicity, respect, and courage to be at the heart of my model is basically a personal one. At the same time, it is the product of an intense learning journey over the last couple of years if not my whole career as manager and consultant. Here is what my favourite values mean to me.

Commitment

What does commitment mean to me? Basically, it means that I am willing to do whatever I can to achieve a specific goal. It is about feeling myself responsible for a certain outcome even if this outcome just makes a small difference as the starfish story suggests.

What's the moral of the starfish story? What does it say about the nature of commitment? On the one hand, it emphasises that commitment is about passion. In business, this passion is making a difference for our customers. On the other hand, we commit ourselves to our team on multiple dimensions such as:

- sharing a mission that is focused on customer value;
- deciding how much work to commit to, balancing demand and capability with regard to sprint length or WIP limit;
- agreeing on who will perform which tasks and making sure all the work is completed;
- sticking to joint definitions of done and explicit policies;
- cultivating a sense of ownership for the value creation process;
- managing ourselves within the given boundaries;
- holding each other accountable and not letting us off the hook if we are in trouble; and
- pursuing continuous improvement on the systemic level as well as on the level of the individual learning journey so that we build on our strengths and recognise our limits in a way that encourages others to help.

Saving starfish

A young boy walks along a beach littered with thousands of starfish. Every couple of meters, he bends down to pick up a starfish and throws it back into the sea. A man watching the boy walks up to him shaking his head and asks, "What are you doing?"

"I'm saving the starfish," the boy answers.

"But that doesn't make any sense," replies the man, bewildered. "What difference does it make to these thousands of other starfish?"

"It makes a difference to this one here," the boy replies, throwing one more starfish into the sea.

Figure 8: When you need help.

Simplicity

What is the simplest thing that could possibly work? In most cases, it is better to do a simple thing today and change it tomorrow if necessary than to do a more complicated thing that takes a week and isn't really needed. Certainly, the balance between "too much complexity" and "enough complexity" remains a tricky one. In this book, Einstein's famous dictum of making things as simple as possible but not simpler is reflected in various ways, for instance by:

- a kind of hands-on theory that risks oversimplification;
- compelling stories and statements;
- a pragmatic approach to capabilities as well as tools (if something works do more of it and if something doesn't work then do something else);
- advocating a sharp business focus and pulling systems based on limited work in progress;

- providing simple models rather than complicated ones;
- using analogies and stories to better illustrate complex phenomena; and
- using metaphors for theory as well as experience.

Unfortunately, simplicity is not a given. It takes time to make something as simple as possible. It took time to write this book (as always, far longer than expected). It takes time to focus on the right things, provide the right organisational design, and facilitate self-organisation. This is underscored by the famous story of French philosopher Blaise Pascal, who apologized for a letter with "I have made this longer than usual because I haven't had the time to make it shorter."

Respect

These days, respect seems to be everybody's cup of tea. As racism, sexism, and homophobia are phenomena you can still observe daily, there are plenty of reasons for respect. Unfortunately, the word has become more of a rhetoric formula than a concrete practice. What does respect mean to me? And how can we detect whether or not respect is part of the common ground of our teamwork?

In a world of cross-functionality, it is a truism that teams comprise different individuals who have been shaped by their specific background and experiences. To me, respect means to treat everybody equally regardless of an individual's knowledge, maturity, gender, sexual orientation, or ethnicity. Even more, respect means to embrace differences as a catalyst for both learning and productivity. The respectful exchange between different experts is at the heart of the C/D/E model for self-organising teams (see "What are self-organising teams?").

Although I think that respect is pretty much about building personal relationships, it also mirrors our relationship to the organisation. We shouldn't forget that respect is a prerequisite of membership. Whether you like it or not, you have to acknowledge basic rules and regulations, fulfil certain expectations, and acclimatise to the corporate culture in order to be respected as a regular member. You will get into trouble rather sooner than later if you are not willing to accept the given boundaries and you question many decisions. Especially when it comes to changing, respect is what makes or breaks your initiative.

How to change things without respect

Many years ago, I was invited to facilitate a workshop with IT project managers about the introduction of agile software development. The message from the external Scrum expert raised a few eyebrows. Project management using the waterfall model, according to him, was dysfunctional and only the agile approach generates business value. Everyone could forget their plans and, certainly, the idea of managing.

It's hardly surprising that I needed to rescue the expert from crucifixion. Equally unsurprising was that his fate was sealed because he questioned everything that the project managers had taken as gospel for so many years. Worse, he completely devalued any previous experience, which generated a lot of resistance. "Just what is he thinking?" one of the project managers said during a break, summing things up. "That we've produced only bull**** up until now?"

This doesn't necessarily mean that you have to treat organisational boundaries as if they were cast in stone. But you have to be able to see these boundaries from a systemic point of view, too. There is always a history behind what we easily criticise, there is at least some sense in what we see as a blockade. In the lean and agile world, many practitioners are quick to see managers as the biggest impediment. Sometimes, this leads to bashing management without realising how this betrays some of our espoused values. How can we aim to respect while generally blaming managers? This does not necessarily mean accepting current dysfunction, but it means acknowledging rather than rejecting culture in the first place. Without this fundamental respect, it's hard to change anything.

Once again, respect is also about myself. It is about how I treat myself, and those I love, in terms of work/life balance, emotional needs, and our respective wishes. No doubt, this is easier said than done. Nevertheless, if it isn't on my radar, I will never achieve any sustainable pace.

Courage

To me, courage includes other important values such as openness, transparency, and feedback. Being courageous means speaking honestly with my teammates and openly showing my work in progress. What results have I achieved so far? What are the areas I am struggling with? What hinders flow? What can we do about it? Instead of creating a black box and working on hidden agendas, I do my best to make everything as explicit as possible.

On the team level, being courageous also means regularly reviewing product as well as process and actively listening to what our stakeholders have to say. Besides, teams should have the courage to build on certain metrics to learn more about the current state of their work system. As I will show in more detail in the chapter on designing, self-organising teams stick to transparency because they want to build on real data and accurate feedback to do the best they can – even if this means questioning what they take for granted.

Figure 9: Improvement is not far from you.

Moreover, courage is closely connected to the principle of regular inspection and adaption. The ability to provide and receive professional feedback is key to self-organisation. As pointed out in the section on commitment, feedback is also a key means by which to hold each other accountable. Without openness about what team members appreciate of each other and where they wish to see more or less of a specific behaviour, there will be no change. This includes the willingness to risk conflict because we know that the positive resolution of these conflicts builds trust.

Last but not least, courage is shown by my willingness to recognise organisational boundaries as well as personal limits. Sometimes, teams cultivate informal whining about dysfunctional structures, inefficient processes, or lacking resources. Courage on this level means to do whatever we can to openly challenge these kinds of impediments – and to truly accept that we cannot change everything at once. We have to respect both systemic and personal limits as Karl Weick and Kathleen Sutcliffe point out in their landmark book on *Managing the Unexpected* (2001, p.123): "It is a sign of strength and confidence to realise when you've reached the limits of your knowledge and know enough to enlist outside help."

Certainly, the four values are not totally separate from each other. Similar to the core capabilities and tools I will present, they are not mutually exclusive categories. On the contrary, they overlap and sometimes even depend on each other. For instance:

- Courage cannot be thought of without respect, a deep sense of responsibility for the decisions you make, and the people affected by them.
- You cannot commit yourself without respect for the organisational context and the courage to make yourself responsible for a certain result.
- Simplicity needs courage to leave things off, make brave decisions, or take some business risks.

Even more importantly, it is definitely not enough to espouse these values. As I will show in the chapters on focusing and changing, espousing values without checking whether they are consistent with organisational artefacts or the team's underlying assumptions is pointless. Because these values are supposed to inspire capabilities as well as tools, consistency is an important factor. In short, we have to assess the corporate culture that surrounds any self-organising team in order to see what is really valued the most.

However, it seems to be the right time to shift the focus from the heart to the head and hands of my simple model, to the four key capabilities of leading self-organising teams and some of my favourite tools in terms of worksheets, questionnaires, and guidelines.

PART
FOUR

Capabilities for leading self-organising teams

Focusing

///////////////////////////

It should not come as surprise that lean and agile approaches focus on customers. Whereas values guide how we make sense of the world, value is what drives our business. Lean thinking sets five building blocks for this business:

1. Identify value from the customer's standpoint.

2. Identify the value stream, the value-creating steps in the process.

3. Create flow, remove delays between those value-creating steps, and eliminate any waste.

4. Establish pull, where work is taken from upstream only in response to downstream demand, ultimately from the customer.

5. Identify waste and remove impediments to smooth flow.

The Agile Manifesto sets a similar priority: satisfying customers through early and continuous delivery of valuable software. Hence, the baseline question for every organisational unit is whether specific decisions or policies help to quickly deliver value to the external customer. Are we truly focused on our customer's needs? Do we consistently create value throughout our work process? Or are we primarily oriented on the interests of a senior manager, internal policy, or formal strategy?

The quote underscores that the starting point for each self-organising team has to be value as defined by the ultimate customer. This definition is only meaningful when expressed in terms of a specific product or a service that is delivered as good and fast as possible. This product, service, or both at once is supposed to meet the customer's needs at a specific price at a specific time. In lean thinking, the value stream is defined as the set of all specific actions required to bring a specific value through all internal process steps to the external customer. Therefore, it should be clear that the core capability of focusing could not be limited to the given boundaries of a team. On the contrary, we have to focus on the end-to-end value stream.

To focus on the value stream is a bit like wearing a pair of eyeglasses that helps you to focus and see what you need to do. All teams should ask themselves whether or not they have this big picture in mind. Do we know how to make a difference for the customer? Are we able to do so? Is it clear how we satisfy our customer's needs and contribute to our organisation's overall success? If in doubt about your answers, the questionnaire might help you to identify your customers and what they care about.

To use an analogy, the value stream is a bit like a river that provides water to thirsty people. The water flows from the source along a path and over rocks and dams until it finally satisfies somebody's thirst. Certainly, the value of satisfying thirst depends both on how long the water flows and on its final quality. From the customer's perspective, it does not make sense to locally optimise the river's flow or cleanliness. If the river is staunched or polluted downstream, it does not make any difference if everything is fine upstream. In order to satisfy thirst as fast as possible, we have to focus on the whole river flow.

Therefore, the ability to identify, map, and continuously improve end-to-end value streams is a key capability for leading self-organising teams. Some teams tend to overlook the importance of value streams as they focus too much on tasks. The creation of a team mission statement is a very effective practice for checking both your understanding of your team's purpose and the specific value you create for your customers. What are you specialising in? What do you deliver? How does a client benefit from it?

Mission statements

Once, I was involved with the IT marketing service department of an Austrian energy provider that made the joint creation of explicit mission statement both a team-building activity and an essential part of a broader reorganisation effort. Although most people had known each other for quite some time, many of them found themselves within new boundaries. At the same time, the focus of the three expert teams was changed in various ways. That's why I was invited to facilitate three one-day workshops to build the teams around powerful mission statements. Later on, a fourth day was invested to align the team missions, check their consistency, and distil a mission for the department as well.

Once you are clear about the mission of your team or department, it pays to spend some time on clarifying your personal vision. What does your idealised future look like? What do you want to achieve in X years? What are your big-picture aspirations for your team/department/organisation? Creating a shared vision statement for your team as suggested in the tools section is a worthwhile investment. It helps you to see the forest for the trees by going beyond the pragmatic sprints and flows of daily business. As Toyota has shown, a powerful vision at the enterprise level provides guidance too. Their "True North", consisting of zero defects, 100% value-added, one-piece flow, in sequence, on demand, and security for people gives direction for all levels of production – individuals as well as teams. Similarly, there are long-term visions for knowledge work. Big, long-term goals such as best service quality, highest customer satisfaction, or best place to work – as set by the IT marketing service department mentioned in the box – are not really achievable. Yet, they state clearly where to head.

Value, waste, and the limits of self-organising teams

If we focus on value, we have to focus on waste as well. Value and waste are two sides of the same coin. In his landmark book *The Principles of Product Development Flow* (2009), Don Reinertsen shows how the linkage of batch size, variability, queues, and constraints contributes to team as well as organisational failure. In most cases, as figure 10 suggests, development resources are wasted through rampant task switching, a high number of blocked work items, centralised control, and bureaucratic resource allocation. Rather than building on regular feedback from the customer, development continues mostly according to a predefined plan.

To manage product development effectively, we must recognize that valuable new information is constantly arriving throughout the development cycle. Rather than remaining frozen in time, locked to our original plan, we must learn to make good economic choices using this emerging information. (*ibid*, p.9)

To make matters worse, not only is new information ignored and an agile response to new demands and shifting contexts neglected. Obsession with plans increases coordination costs through an overwhelming number of handovers and alignment meetings. Let alone that many of these meetings miss professional management and facilitation.

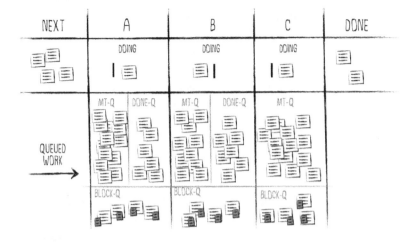

Figure 10: Queues for task switching, done work, and blocked work on a Kanban board

The bottom line of all this is high risks and low profits. Instead of flow, many teams are busy managing congestion. To overcome all these troubles, Reinertsen's economic framework for product development emphasises small batch transfers, limited work in progress, and rapid feedback. Flow can be smoothed by different strategies such as:

- limiting the number of parallel activities to reduce cycle times;
- establishing a pull system rather than push;
- making value-driven decisions, e.g. by moving items with the highest cost of delay to the head of the line;
- focusing on problems and constraints that hinder flow;
- establishing clear policies for queuing discipline;
- defining a cadence of meetings for synchronisation and feedback; and
- making work as well as workflow visible (you can find more about these strategies and how to model them in the chapter on designing).

The **inability to see the impact of queues** is often worsened by focusing exclusively on functional or team-level performance. By applying push systems, the value stream is hindered if not blocked in many ways. While we are working on an item, we have many items waiting below the waterline of our activity: multitasking items we actively work on every now and then; items that are blocked for various reasons; and done work we haven't yet pushed forward. In short, we simply have too much work in our system. Therefore, we manage a traffic jam rather than flow. From a lean perspective, any self-organising team has to understand how the work they manage works, and then focus on how to make it better. They need to design their work system for the better, as we will show in more detail in the next chapter. This is not to say that teams must know all the answers. Nor must managers. The critical thing is that they know what questions to ask. And they know how to process them, which is, as we will see later on, also a matter of professional facilitation.

Reducing waste

Mary and Tom Poppendieck tell a nice story that explains why reducing waste is also a matter of timely responses: "It's the same as losing your keys: if you lost them a few seconds ago, look down. If you lost them a few minutes ago, retrace your steps. If you lost them a week ago, change the locks. And yet we wait until the end of the development process to test our code, and by that time we need a lot of locksmiths." (Poppendieck 2010, p.71)

Many lean and agile practitioners see handovers as one of the biggest wastes in product development. Handovers occur whenever we separate

- responsibility (what to do);
- knowledge (how to do it);
- action (doing the work); and
- feedback (learning from the results).

Paradoxically, a critical review of this separation is most often seen as a waste of time, let alone experiments in managing work more holistically. As a matter of fact, most businesses are still managed by **looking at single data points** instead of a series of data in context. We measure individual performance, lead times of single work items, management efficiency, cost of individual services, and so on. Although we should know better, we try to maximise local performance – e.g. the performance of individual experts and functional silos – and ignore that we thereby most often sub-optimise overall performance. This explains why we cannot limit self-organisation to the boundaries of a single team. Once we orient ourselves on customer value, the focus of leadership must always be on the plural. Even if we manage just one team, we have to lead with an eye on the other teams as well. In the changing chapter, I will show that this holds especially true for all efforts to improve the performance of self-organising systems.

Awareness, a dangerous ladder, and the illusion of skill

And what is the morale of the story of the lost keys? As far as I am concerned, there are at least two conclusions to be drawn: first, **focusing needs awareness**, the ability to mindfully scan what is going in your system and in its environment; second, have the ability to scan unexpected events such as individual defects, moving targets, or general shifts in customer demand. To a degree, the future is always opaque, but it's a lot more so if you close your eyes.

Focusing is a complex capability that encompasses an appropriate perception of your customers (needs and demands), your current organisational system (value stream and containers), your team's structure and dynamics (differences and exchange), and last but not least yourself.

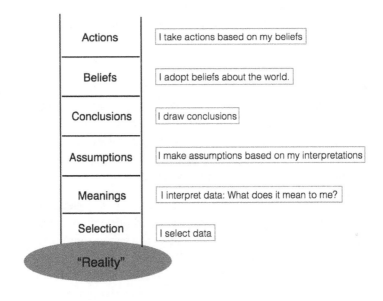

Figure 11: The ladder of inference.

Why do we need to be aware of ourselves? If we do not mindfully scan what is going on inside us, we build our actions on assumptions and beliefs rather than data and experience. As Chris Argyris's famous "Ladder of Inference" shows (figure 11), we reflexively select data from reality, which we then interpret (Argyris 1999). A classic example is the traditional process of management reporting. Usually, the report is limited to pure facts apart from any context or process. Hence, management's focus is on results, milestones, costs, and the like. However, the presented figures and numbers get interpreted: "What does it mean if one result is X? How does this result resonate with milestone Y? What if we've only achieved Z instead of ZZ?" Based on the added meaning, managers make certain assumptions and draw conclusions such as "If we compare X with Y, we recognise that there is need for action!" Most of the time, management's assumptions and conclusions confirm their general beliefs. Even more, these beliefs guide the specific actions that will be taken. For instance, "We have to send team X on training," "We will definitely bring in more people to help," "We must limit the scope of project Z," and so on.

Usually, all of this happens within a few fractions of a second – and it happens without effort. Moreover, we are neither aware of the ladder nor of the wobbly ground it sits on. We hide our selective perception, we ignore how we bridge the gaps between our perception and the reality around us, and we are not aware of the consequences of this practice. Dietrich Dörner's famous analysis, *The Logic of Failure* (1996), reminds us of these consequences.

Fortunately, the logic of failure is no fate. We can change the way we act, we can increase our levels of awareness, and we can more broadly apply systems thinking. Reconstructing how we climb up the Ladder of Inference is a good starting point for this learning journey. The worksheet in "Catch you if you can" (see "Tools for focusing") could help you to gain some insights and improve your awareness.

Unfortunately, this is not the only area where we selectively perceive, draw possibly wrong conclusions, and build our actions on questionable assumptions. The notorious knowing-doing gap is another example that haunts managers as well as teams. Basically, this gap is the product of a rationality myth. Simply speaking, we believe that we are able to really do what we capture cognitively. For instance, we understand that self-organisation depends on an empowering container. We know that we must not micro-manage our teams. We agree to the idea of decentralised control and clear decision-making authorities. We even know why we should stick to empowering actions and refrain from non-supportive ones. Yet, our practices tell another story. In many cases, we do not practice what we preach. That's why "walk the talk" has become just another example for the rampant leadership rhetoric.

The logic of failure

Untested assumptions not only produce short-sightedness but also have concrete consequences. The essence of Dörner's analysis (1996) is that through leaping into action, overdoing established measures, or denying side effects, our action itself becomes the problem. Unfortunately, many organisations would rather play around with familiar symptoms than look for causes as yet unknown to them.

We act without thinking of systemic effects.

We do not consider long-term effects and side effects. Instead, we tend to overdo established measures, particularly under time constraints.

We ignore processes by controlling static conditions rather than dynamic interactions.

We can solve what we can rather than what we should.

We apply expertism, which can tempt us to overestimate our own abilities or to transgress safety standards.

We act without organisational awareness and carry out isolated projects without considering systemic needs for change.

We neglect critical self-reflection and evade uncertainty through denial or delegation of the problem.

Where does the knowing-doing gap come from? And how can we bridge if not overcome this gap? Nobel laureate Daniel Kahneman identifies a widespread "illusion of skill" that leads to chronic overestimation of our capabilities. Need a striking example? According to a recent Wall Street Journal survey of 1,100 British first-line managers, a full 72% of those questioned never doubt their own leadership capabilities. Furthermore, 80% of them would place themselves among the most successful top 20% of managers. There is, as Kahneman puts it, "a puzzling limitation of our mind: our excessive confidence in what we believe we know, and our apparent inability to acknowledge the full extent of our ignorance and the uncertainty of the world we live in." (Kahneman 2011, p.14)

Managers tend to overlook both this inability and the necessity to continuously improve the ways they deal with uncertainty and risk.

Speaking of this blind spot, the famous question about the difference between great athletes and managers pops up again. What separates them is primarily the difference between the time spent in practice and the time spent in competition. Great athletes invest a huge amount of time in their training regimes and much less in the competitions themselves. The focus of all exceptional athletes is on preparation. This is the phase when the essentials for the whole season and the foundations for the desired success are laid. It is the other way round with managers, who barely train at all and spend all their time in competition instead.

Zen mastery

"What shall I do?" the Zen apprentice asks his master while standing in front of a tall ladder.

"You can climb the ladder, rung by rung, to the top."

"How many rungs does the ladder have?" asks the apprentice.

"Eighteen," the Zen master replies.

"And what should I do when I'm at the top?" the apprentice wants to know as he places his foot on the first rung.

"You can stand there," the master explains in a friendly manner, "you can enjoy the view, you can climb back down, or you can continue to climb without any rungs."

Once again, the Toyota way to lean leadership may serve as an example for learning through repetition to achieve both a profound understanding and practice. Rather than dreaming of charisma that will make people follow them, managers must commit themselves to a life-long journey in self-development. In addition to developing themselves, they have to develop others once they have gained enough experience to allow coaching and mentoring. The story about the Zen master and his apprentice provides a nice analogy for this kind of journey. The questionnaire in the tool section provides a pragmatic opportunity to quickly assess your current commitment to self-development.

Knowing-doing gaps to focus on

A good way to bridge the knowing-doing gap is to establish a system for consistent training, best on or near the job to allow for fast feedback. In the upcoming chapters, I will show that we have to design for and professionally facilitate a broad variety of feedback loops.

In a self-organising environment, the focus must be on continuous development rather than training or a workshop every now and then. Moreover, all practice is worthless if there is no honest feedback that helps us to see whether we're improving. Without establishing a system of fast feedback loops, we can neither make sure that we are doing the right thing nor get fresh impulses on what we can do even better.

Although the commitment to consistent self-development is a catalyst for overcoming the illusion of skill, to focus only on the personal level does not guarantee continuous improvement in a self-organising environment. We need team and organisation development, too. Today, it seems to be a truism that teams are not the sum of their parts but the product of their interaction. Yet in many organisations I have worked with, team building was seen more as a matter of singular events than as a development process over a longer period of time.

As a matter of fact, professional development of self-organising teams in terms of consistently realising the full potential of a group of cross-functional experts is anything but a given. Again, the world of sports shows that teams have to train as teams, not as individuals, in order to build both the right mind-set and proper techniques for smooth interaction. As the C/D/E model suggests, teams have to start with trustfully exploring their differences to make the best out of their diversity. Lee Gardenswartz and Anita Rowe's statements for sharing perspectives on the team are a good catalyst for this kind of exchange (see page 91). The suggested pair structure for this kind of sharing creates a safe container for open exchange and building trust. Professionally facilitated, it helps team members to build trust and creates a stable foundation for holding each other accountable. Step by step, the team members overcome their proverbial blindness and explore the whole elephant.

Figure 12: Exploring the whole elephant.

Effective collaboration is not something that evolves automatically. Whether you apply the famous "-orming" model (forming, storming, norming, performing) or any other concept to monitor your team's development, you cannot build on any "natural growth" that happens just by doing business together. On the contrary, I have encountered many teams that were still struggling with basic policies after more than a year of working together. Specialists who are supposed to be effectively working in and as a team often are primarily focused on their individual expertise. Once, a manager of a second-level support team called me in to help with "pushing performance". After conversations with team members and the product owner, I found out that the whole IT department was reorganised and the team newly staffed three times within six months. No wonder that this team was not performing as expected since they were still busy with their initial setup.

But what is actually needed to build a performing team? How can we support self-organisation in a consistent way? Where should we focus if we want to create a culture of continuous improvement of both individuals and groups? Similar to the personal level, teams also need to continuously practice and regularly review what they have achieved and where they still need to focus. The world of lean and Agile development provides many good formats for this kind of looping:

- stand-ups for operational coordination;
- product reviews for continuous delivery and customer feedback;
- operations reviews to focus on metrics and impediments, internally and/or with the team's stakeholders;
- retrospectives to inspect and adapt the process of collaboration at all levels;
- team-building events to clarify, calibrate, or fine-tune interactions;
- innovation workshops, e.g. for rapid prototyping with external customers (for more formats and how to design them see the chapter on facilitating);
- pair programming or other pair approaches to prompt fresh impulses and increase the quality of achievements; and
- peer coaching to help each other on or near the job.

The greatest enemy of communication is the illusion of it

A couple of years ago, I facilitated a workshop with the top managers of an online-entertainment company. Officially, we were there to strengthen teamwork and agree on real steps for improvement.

As it turned out, there was less talking done with each other and far more with no one in particular. We were occupied for endless hours with clarifying accountabilities and responsibilities in a complicated matrix structure.

Unsurprisingly, things got pretty heated in this micro-political arena. Everyone interrupted; few listened to anything. My attempts to professionally facilitate failed. We couldn't find an exit from this arena and got stuck in a pointless discussion at the content level rather than moving to the relationship level to address the obvious lack of trust. Communication became a complete illusion.

On the other hand, many of these formats are focused on daily business as if the world only consists of a series of sprints, iterations, or increments. Even though daily business must be at the centre of our attention, we have much more room to discover improvement. The guidelines on levels of team communication (see page 92) will kindly remind you that you need more than operational communication to realise the full potential of your team. However, the following story emphasises that we shouldn t take communication for granted.

The team's boundaries have to allow for focusing on the big picture, too, like strategic topics such as product or service development, organisational change, or customer innovation. Likewise, the team's norms should encourage a well-balanced self-reflection in terms of appreciation as well as constructive criticism.

In systems theory, communication goes hand in hand with making decisions. Since we know that the greatest enemy of communication is the illusion of it, regularly checking the quality of your decision-making processes helps a lot. Are you sure that everybody understands what your decision-making policy looks like? Is management clear enough in its role as the boundary keeper of any self-organising team? Is the team aware of what they are entitled to and responsible for? The guidelines on decision-making policies (see page 93) should help you to answer these questions in regard with your current situation.

In general, I think the maturity of self-organising teams is reflected in their ability to go beyond the usual boundaries. In order to respond to the on-going change around us in an agile manner, we have to be able to effectively manage the unexpected. Organisational psychologists Karl Weick and Kathleen Sutcliffe provide us with excellent guidelines for how to cultivate self-control and agile decision-making by acting in anticipation as well as by containing the unexpected when it occurs (Weick and Sutcliffe 2001). There is no doubt that strategies such as moving authority toward expertise wherever it lies for each situation, making relative the meaning of hierarchy and seniority, and focusing on surprises support self-organisation in many ways (see page 95).

What does "managing the unexpected" mean for IT practitioners? What can these strategies look like in lean and Agile teams? It could mean:

- not to limit retrospectives to sprints or any other cadence of product development;
- to regularly inspect and adapt to the bigger picture;
- to look for patterns of interaction, positive ones but also questionable ones that need more than one sprint to develop;

- to monitor the development process as a team over a longer period of time;
- to align their own learning with other teams, especially those working within the same value stream;
- to facilitate joint retrospectives across team and hierarchical boundaries to address organisational issues; and
- to actively involve themselves in entrepreneurial topics such as vision or strategy.

Recently, I had the opportunity to facilitate a series of team events in a German online company. We ran five one-day events with five different Scrum or Kanban teams, encompassing the whole area of engineering. What intrigued me was more than the workshop specific to each team, which focused on their current situation and concrete measures to improve on in the future. The meta-level retrospectives we ran provided a great opportunity to address bigger issues such as:

- issues across teams, e.g. about certain dependencies and the impediments they caused;
- issues about learning more from each other, e.g. about the application of XP, Scrum, and Kanban or technical challenges;
- issues across functional silos such as the tensions between product managers, developers, and UX experts;
- issues concerning the collaboration between the team and the management;
- issues regarding the "big picture" in terms of roadmap and middle-term strategy; and, last but not least,
- issues about how to involve the customer earlier and more effectively.

Since these events were coordinated, they provided an excellent means to explore the proverbial elephant from different points of view. Moreover, they opened the opportunity for focused follow-up sessions at the inter-team level as well as at the level of hierarchy-bridging communication. Even more, the team events provided rich input both for a longer-term development plan for each team in 2015 and for the management team. It is no surprise to me that the management team focused themselves on feedback and leadership, especially on how all the different leaders in their self-organising environment are supposed to play together. Questions such as "Is it clear what leadership means to us?", "Do we know who is in charge for what?", and "Do we play together effectively?" are far from trivial. The first answers have already cast a light on where management has to focus on in 2015.

Corporate culture gaps

What final conclusion can we draw from the various knowing-doing gaps? Perhaps we can conclude that awareness needs to encompass customer demand, process quality, one's own needs and the team's dynamics. Be aware of how you model the behaviours you want to see in place – and set aside time to critically reflect on your actions on a regular basis. Unfortunately, we're not done with being aware of all those things that nurture self-organising processes. In any organisation, there is a much more powerful regime in place that guides all actions, feelings, and thoughts like the famous "invisible hand": your corporate culture.

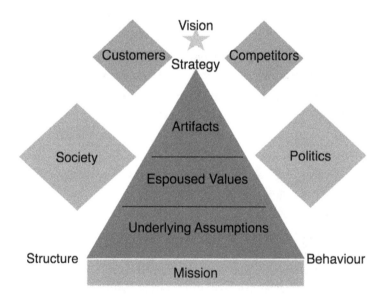

Figure 13: A model of corporate culture.

What is corporate culture about? Organisation and leadership guru Ed Schein provides a definition to overcome the popular tendency to put culture in homogeneous boxes (Schein 2004). Figure 13 helps us better understand the complex nature of corporate culture with the following emphasis:

- It is strongly influenced by the context of the organisational system. In a certain way, corporate culture mirrors the market situation, political climate, or social regulations of its environment.

- It is driven by a particular mission, a specific organisational purpose, and is oriented towards a particular vision.

- It shapes and is shaped by a triangle of goals and strategies (a.k.a. objectives), structures (a.k.a. organisation design), and behaviour (a.k.a. interactions).

- It can be subdivided into three levels:

  - artefacts, i.e. all phenomena that you can see, hear, or feel such as the architecture, products, processes, routines, and spirit of an organisation;

  - espoused values, i.e. all messages that are supposed to guide the organisation's strategies for achieving its goals like "We focus particularly on...", "We emphasise...", "What is important to us" etc., as well as the values presented to the outside world: "We stand for..."; "We represent..."; "We handle XYZ in the following way..."; etc.

  - basic assumptions, which, largely as subconscious, self-evident stipulations, form the parameters for actual behaviour. What does management really expect? What behaviour do my colleagues appreciate? What has the team done before that paid off? What is the natural way of doing things around here?

Figure 14: What is culture?

Ed Schein uses a wonderful metaphor to explain this nature: culture is what makes us feel at home, just like water for a fish. Hence, as figure 14 shows, we're pretty surprised when asked to describe this completely natural state of affairs.

Why bother with corporate culture in a book about leading self-organising teams? I think there are a few good reasons. To start with a simple argument, we could refer to the truism that context is always king. A self-organising team is not like the proverbial Gallic village. As shown, a self-organising team inevitably depends on an organisational environment that cannot be reduced to "bad Romans". Far more than setting only formal, potentially dysfunctional boundaries, the broader environment in terms of management and organisational design highly influences how we feel about our work and about working in the team. We should not forget that corporate culture also shapes supposedly personal things like self-esteem, confidence, and pride. Moreover, Schein's model explains why an existing non-supportive culture such as one based on command and control can't all that easily change. Corporate culture is a deep, broad, and relatively stable phenomenon that has often grown over a long period of time. After all, bureaucratic and hierarchical systems still represent the collective capability and wisdom of its members: in other words, the experience, thoughts, and feelings that have made these systems successful (or at least helped them to survive).

From a systemic viewpoint, the crucial question is whether or not the existing culture is functional for leading self-organising teams. Simply ask to what extent does our culture promote the strategies, structures, and behaviours that will let us successfully realise the full potential of self-organisation. But how can we detect whether our corporate culture promotes or hinders self-organisation? How can we find out what makes or breaks our team's success?

There is good news to start with: even though corporate culture is for the most part based on underlying, partly subconscious assumptions, it is neither inaccessible nor unchangeable. As always, answering the question of what the current culture looks like must start with a shared understanding of what we are talking about and why this talk is important. I have experience with leading a good, simple exercise designed by Ed Schein. This exercise allows you to briefly assess your cultural DNA in order to agree on what to build upon and what to change for a better future (see the guidelines in "Deciphering your company culture", page 96).

In summary, what makes or breaks the success of self-organising teams is cultural consistency. Do the official values support leadership as a team sport? Do these values resonate with how people run their daily business? How is lean or agile mirrored on the artefact level, e.g. by finance or HR processes? Often, the cultural pulse is plagued by all kinds of dysfunction. This happens mainly because contradictions between artefacts and espoused values are neglected.

> ### Some real-life scenarios
>
> I was once involved with the software-development department of an energy provider that wanted to go agile. In meetings, enthusiastic managers spoke of openness and courage although the employees still sat in small cubicles with their doors permanently shut. Meetings were mainly used for one-way information, change thought took a top-down driven approach, and workshops were a space for analysis-paralysis.
>
> Within the already mentioned telco, the importance of communication was emphasised at all official occasions. At the same time, informal exchange was labelled as mere chitchat. Strategy development was a privilege of senior managers: product development was something to be pushed by functional experts, also known as an "ivory-tower bridge".
>
> In one business unit of a big insurance company, collaboration was heralded as a key value. Nevertheless, nothing was done to establish it at a silo or hierarchy-bridging level. Instead of involving employees in decision-making processes, the so-called management team was very busy figuring out what was called "the commander's intent for the troops".

Consider the scenarios in the box below. Similar cultural contradictions are evident between espoused values and concrete behaviour. Peter Hundermark and I have stated that "culture eats Agile for breakfast" (Kaltenecker 2013), summarising lessons we've learned in various organisations.

Once we have identified such contradictions, we can ask ourselves if we want to change them. What kind of dysfunction does this contradiction represent? What are its current and potential future business impacts? Where does the dysfunction come from? What's the value of overcoming it? The moment we better understand the real problem, its consequences for business as well as morale, and the respective root causes, we can start looking for possible solutions. For this solution-oriented process, we can use some of the methods in the chapter on facilitating. And if we have an effective change system in place, it should neither be hard to prioritise possible improvement actions nor to monitor their flow – as the chapter on changing will show. Before that, I still have to clarify what focusing means for another core capability: the organisational design of both our particular teams and our whole enterprise.

Culture eats agile for breakfast

A Swiss online company praised the virtues of self-organised teamwork although they still based all rewards and control systems on individual responsibility. This suggested that it was the individual and not the team that really counted.

A big German bank officially supported diversity management and equality programs while completely ignoring structural phenomena such as the income gap between men and women, career disadvantages for migrants, and the rejection of older employees. This again leads one to conclude that the work of young, white, native-born men is still valued more highly.

An Austrian car supplier valued the perspectives of employees by regularly asking for leadership feedback. At the same time, this feedback was reduced to anonymous surveys, which said a lot about organisational trust and the willingness to hold each other accountable.

A South African IT-services provider emphasised decentralised decision-making and control. On the other hand, team decisions were overruled in many situations and a new system for performance control was about to be implemented.

Designing

////////////////////////

It is a popular misconception that self-organisation means "just doing our own thing". On the contrary, self-organising teams need the right organisational design to thrive. From an organisational point of view, as shown in the "Self-organising teams" chapter, they need:

clear boundaries in terms of direction, team setup, and decision-making policies;

supportive context in terms of a proper infrastructure, encouraging information, education, and reward systems; and

an empowering culture that guides individual exchanges, the joint commitment to challenging goals, and mutual help in terms of knowledge sharing, coaching, and learning.

In talking about eliminating waste, we should not forget that we have to **give up managing people's activities, too**. On the one hand, it is simply an incredible waste of management resource: instead of being empowered by clear boundaries and supportive context, most teams are still micro-managed. On the other hand, and probably even worse, this style of management demoralises workers: rather than having the autonomy they deserve and need to thrive, they are held under the regime of traditional command and control. Instead of empowering self-organisation, micro-management is a popular strategy for committing what Tom DeMarco and Timothy Lister (1999) call **"teamicide"**. What they say about the relationship between management and highly performing teams resonates with my concept of self-organising teams.

Sometimes it's murder – death by intent to kill: high-performance teams often achieve what they achieve by breaking the rules of the prevailing corporate culture. Managers can feel threatened and so they disband them, in order to preserve the status quo. Sometimes it's manslaughter – death by negligence: the management doesn't understand the high-performance team or its mode of operation and so it does things that unintentionally eliminate high-performance, e.g. moving members of a high-performance team to other teams, ostensibly with the goal of creating more high-performance teams but typically with the result of eliminating any high performance. (*ibid*, p.14)

In summary, it can be stated that the design of most organisations is still focused on managing people and activities. But we need macro-management rather than micro-management to effectively shift the relationship between managers and self-organising teams from an adversarial hierarchy to a complementary one. You can use the brief self-assessments on page 99 and page 109 to better understand your own balance between micro and macro perspectives.

How can we design for macro-management? How do we set the right focus? What do the right team and role setups look like? Once again, systems thinking helps us to answer these questions. As mentioned, to take a systems view is to think about the organisation from the outside in, to understand customer demand and to design a system that meets it. Self-organisation and self-control are key for such a design. To enable this it is necessary, as John Seddon puts it (2008, p.78), "to integrate decision-making with work (so the workers control the work) and use measures derived from the work…. If workers are controlling the work, they need managers to be working on the things beyond the control of the workers which affect the system conditions: the way work works. The result is an adaptive, customer-centric system." If workers fully control both the management and the monitoring of their work, they need managers to work on the things beyond their control. Hence, managers work on the system whereas team members work in the system.

Visual work management with kanban

What can such a system design look like? I have much experience with all kinds of visual work-management systems. Figure 15 shows the basic structure of such a system. It is a sketch of a simple kanban board that builds on some of the key practices defined by David Anderson (Anderson 2010): visualisation, WIP limits, and workflow.

Why this design? Basically, it helps us to capture a lot of things in one glance:

- what the work system looks like;
- what work we have in our system (the small tickets);

- how work flows (from the input column over the process steps A to C to the done column);
- what is in "doing" and what is "done" and ready to be pulled forward from one process step to the next (picture, for instance, analysis-development-test in classic software development);
- which work is blocked (the small red sticky notes on certain tickets); and
- how parallel activities are limited in order to foster flow (the numbers on top that indicate the of maximum number of tickets in each column).

The purpose of making things as transparent as possible is twofold. Mike Burrows explains (2014, p.7) that the reasons are "…to make the need for action visible and to help people make good choices. These operate at two levels: Action in the form of work that needs to be done; good choices in the selection of work items; Action in the form of changes to the system; good choices in justifying, scoping, and implementing change."

Figure 15: A sketch of a kanban board.

In addition to making visible what is often invisible in knowledge work, most self-organising teams make the implicit explicit. Written policies summarise how to handle the system and what behaviours the team members expect of each other. Rules about ticket design and how to pull tickets are as common as rules about dealing with blockades or the notorious white noise. Everything necessary to successfully operate the visual work-management system is jointly defined in a self-organising manner.

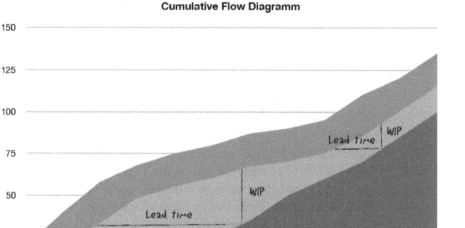

Figure 16: A simple cumulative-flow diagram.

Although helpful, pure visual management is not enough to bring forth any improvements. A board merely sheds light on the current situation. Once again, you need to establish a system of effective feedback loops to optimise your system. Usually, visually managed teams have a mixture of meetings and metrics to identify and solve problems, start experiments, and get real data to see whether they are improving or not. Everything is kept as simple as possible: meetings are short and disciplined, metrics easy to use and interpret. Figure 16 shows a simple cumulative-flow diagram, often used to better understand the linkage between WIP limits and lead times (cornflower blue = number of tickets to do, green = doing, blue = done). Other teams use histograms, spectral analysis, and blockade clusters to measure their performance. In the chapter on facilitating, I show how to design typical agile and kanban meetings, and how to moderate them in order to encourage, as the fourth kanban principle states, leadership at all levels.

Many self-organising teams use visual work management in the form of task or flow boards, burn-down or burn-up charts, histograms, or cumulative-flow diagrams. All these visualisations use colour and simple symbols to provide relevant information in one picture. Most often, visual management manifests itself in physical boards with coloured sticky notes and tape to structure the flow of work.

Some teams also take extra time to come up with a so-called team charter (see the guidelines on page 101). Similar to a mission statement, the team charter is a written summary of the key pillars of a self-organising team. In addition to a pure mission statement, it encompasses all relevant information on organisational design and processes. It answers basic questions such as "What is most important to us, fulfilling our mission?", "What do we value most, working on this team?", "How do we organise ourselves?", "What are key policies of our work?", and "How do we measure whether we are doing a good job as a team?" A professionally created team charter:

- encourages conversation and common understanding;
- summarises important agreements with key stakeholders;
- ensures knowledge of organisational constraints that are not within the authority of a single team like IT governance, regulatory constraints, or delivery dates in a scaled environment; and
- helps new team members to familiarise themselves with the team.

Figure 17 brings us back to the big picture of visual work management. The example of an IT department of a South African insurance company shows what a kanban board can look like in real life.

Again, you find all the elements mentioned before: visualised work process (columns, separated by black tape); work items (coloured cards), policies (A4 sheets on top of the columns); and avatars (small stickers on the cards) to show which part of the organisation had requested the work item. These stickers were added to make the feedback part easier.

The board also shows what different types of work are in the system. Green cards are "epics" or large story buckets. These were actually envelopes, inside which yellow story cards were placed until worked on. We also see how many stories we have at each stage of completion. Finally, the horizontal swim lanes are split per team. That's how we can tell what each group is working on, and prevents overloading the teams.

The board underscores that visual work management is the process of making useful information obvious. It makes visible your current performance customer demands visible and helps to make your jobs easier by:

- bringing relevant information together;
- making it explicit;
- keeping it updated to keep control and overview;
- identifying problems and constraints in your work process;
- focusing communication;
- enabling better and more predictable choices; and
- encouraging continuous improvement.

Figure 17: A kanban board in a South African insurance company.

Success stories

Success stories were prominently exhibited in the IT department of an international energy firm. After a workshop on the planned global reorganisation, we created a template that all participants were to use to review their change steps:

- What is this change step about?
- Who is its sponsor?
- Which stakeholders are involved?
- What has been achieved?
- What's planned next?

The answers had to include images, screenshots, or quotations in order to make the story as comprehensible as possible. These success stories were exhibited like a public gallery during a department meeting two months later. The department manager who had co-created the template officially opened the exhibition. All could follow their own curiosity, investigate the stories individually, and discuss them with one another. Within a short time, the room was filled with positive storytelling, and feelings of enthusiasm and optimism reigned. "Only now do I know how much positive change can take place!" said one participant, affirming the purpose of the meeting. "And that also changes my perception of improvement steps that didn't work, or haven't yet."

Making things as visible and explicit as possible is not limited to kanban. The above true story shows how it can be used to emphasise a positive approach to collaboration and inspire knowledge sharing between different self-organising teams.

Pull versus push, WIP limits, and measurements

It should not come as a surprise that these features encourage self-organisation at many levels. The visualisation helps to align different points of view and creates a common understanding of our daily business. It emphasises ownership since the workers are supposed to be in the driver's seat when designing their system. Leadership as a team sport is realised from the very beginning by jointly visualising what the team does now and finding better ways to operate in the future. Later on, operating within the system, internal communication is encouraged by proven meeting formats and external communication takes place through transparency and meetings that explicitly address stakeholder's concerns. Visual change-management systems build on self-control by overviewing on a daily basis and applying metrics that make sense for the team and their environment. The visible and explicit nature of knowledge work makes it easier to make the right decisions. In summary, visual work-management systems empower a culture of continuous improvement.

All these positive features depend highly on the right boundaries nevertheless. First and foremost, the effective coordination of input and output is business-critical. On the one hand, the system has to be protected against overwhelming demand; on the other hand, the customer only notices a positive difference if we think end to end, even though your team may only be responsible for a small part of the value chain. Once again, the work system cannot be properly designed without taking its environment into account.

Figure 18: The right design for your environment?

Limiting work in progress is key for this boundary setting. It is not rocket science for lean thinkers to figure out that parallel tasks negatively affect the workflow: the greater the number of work items in the system and the higher their variability, the higher the lead times. By rule of economic thumb, it is much better to work on one work item 100% of the time until it's finished rather than complete 10% of 10 items in the same timeframe. Therefore, in order to reduce the lead times and establish a continuous workflow, you must limit the number of operations carried out simultaneously at any given stage. Hence we talk about limiting work in progress (WIP) known simply as WIP limits.

By the same token, WIP limits help to establish a pull rather than a push system. Traditional push systems are characterised by two features: pushing a predetermined plan, and tracking task completion against that plan; and pushing work from one process step ("functional silo") to the next without bothering about the quality of handovers. Since the plan and the capacities of the different silos are all fixed, a push system is ill equipped to handle variability and change, let alone problems and constraints.

Pull systems, on the other hand, are characterised by a limited amount of parallel work, clear priorities, and commitment to control workflow instead of people and activities. When people want to know what to do next, they pull an item off the top of a prioritised queue. Since these queues can freely change, pull systems are capable of handling variability as well as unexpected problems. Together with minimising capital tied up in the process and reducing lead times, limiting the WIP brings a further advantage that is directly related to the goal of continuous improvement: in a WIP-limited pull system, bottlenecks become visible.

Due to their strong focus on customer value, Kanban systems continuously encourage optimisation of the workflow. Everything that hampers the flow of work, such as blockages and bottlenecks, receives particular attention. The motto is, perhaps, "work on your problems before you pull in new work." Furthermore, we want to be able to stick to the agreements we make with our stakeholders. In order to keep promises and honour agreements, we must know precisely what we're capable of achieving. That's why most kanban practitioners apply metrics to better understand their true capabilities.

Measuring results has a bad reputation with many self-organising teams. For decades, it has been one of the favourite tools of traditional command-and-control management, so many lean and agile practitioners are sceptical if not outright resistant to metrics. As the saying goes, you cannot learn without measurements, but you can measure without learning. However, this feels a bit like throwing out the proverbial baby with the bathwater. Measurement guru Douglas Hubbard argues (2014) that we should not measure for the sake of measuring. On the contrary, we should use metrics as a means to a specific end: namely, to achieve a significant reduction of uncertainty that can be expressed quantitatively.

In order to lead effectively, we have to focus on measurements that are relevant if not critical to key decisions. That's why teams have to bother with measurements. There is no way to encourage leadership at all levels without quantitative feedback on your performance. The main point here is that self-organising teams should have the authority to define what and how to measure for themselves as well as for their most relevant stakeholders. What are key metrics for recognising whether we are doing a good job? How does the customer benefit from these measurements? How do they help us to make the right decisions?

As it turns out, we can actually measure anything we care about. As outlined in the guidelines on page 102, Hubbard provides a simple approach with three basic questions:

- Whenever you think about measuring something, the first question to ask is "What do you mean by (whatever you want to measure)?"
- Why do you care about (whatever you want to measure)?
- What do you expect to observe when (whatever you want to measure) takes place? If it matters at all, it is detectable as an amount and thus can be measured. "If you can define the outcome you really want, give examples of it, and identify how those consequences are observable, then you can design measurements that will measure the outcomes that matter." (*ibid*, p.51)

When we change something, we want to be able to see whether the change proves to be of value. We must measure the impact of our change effort. However, to the relief of all sceptics of traditional metrics, in visual work-management systems, we do not measure the performance of individual employees but the performance of the whole system. We want to examine whether we have developed our capabilities. If we cannot prove any real improvement of our processes, we must change them again. This is how we establish a fast, predictable, and consistent workflow that is the foundation of any kaizen culture. As shown in the chapter on focusing, simple tools such as histograms, spectral analysis, or cumulative-flow diagrams are enough to get real data to learn from.

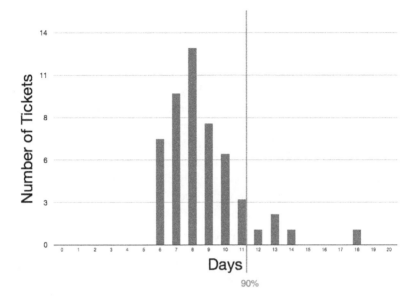

Figure 19: A simple histogram showing the lead times of tickets.

Change and management with kanban

As with lean and agile methods in general, **visual work management is simple in concept but often difficult to execute well**. It takes understanding and agreement, effort and discipline, professionalism and consistency. In short, it depends on both your understanding and your practice of leadership and change management.

This raises at least two important questions. First, how do we properly introduce visual work management? Second, what does this mean for the traditional management role? The answer to the first question is that we should be clear from the very beginning that introducing visual work management means running a change initiative. Together with Klaus Leopold, I have defined a simple process for such an initiative, consisting of four steps (Leopold and Kaltenecker 2015):

• general clarification;

- deeper understanding;

- system design; and

- system operation.

As I further explain in the chapter on changing, these four steps are in line with the "start with what you do now" principle of evolutionary change management. This principle might encourage you to simply visualise what you are doing right now. There is nothing wrong with this approach. Yet building on our experience in various change initiatives with multiple clients, Klaus and I recommend a slightly different approach. For now, it should be enough to provide you a questionnaire that helps to clarify where you actually start when you think about designing your own visual work-management system (see page 103).

Often, this simple questionnaire has helped to catalyse an intense conversation among those willing to invest in systemic change. Regardless of the organisational level of your envisioned kanban implementation – team, department, end-to-end value stream, or portfolio – you should take time to clarify open questions as well as potential blind spots. There is more to come once you realise that you need to accurately identify and involve your most important stakeholders in order to achieve a deeper understanding of your current situation. I will come back to these issues in the chapter on changing. However, you need to fulfil certain prerequisites in order to design a proper visual work-management system. The checklist on page 105 should allow you an overview of these prerequisites. I highly recommend you work through the complete list before you proceed with the design guidelines as you model your own kanban system.

Now to the second question.... What does 21st-century line management look like? I have already shown how to design your work system as well as the self-organising team that runs this system. I have also shown how these designs encourage leadership at many levels, emphasising an understanding of leadership as a team sport rather than as command-and-control regime. But I haven't yet shown what this means for the role of the traditional manager. How do we redesign this role to fit into a lean and agile environment that builds on self-organising processes?

It shouldn't come as a surprise that this fitness has to start with a common understanding of your current management system.

Counterintuitive insights

I remember a stand-up meeting in front of the Kanban board at a Czech service provider. The team had invited one of the product managers as a special guest. Focusing on flow as well on what hinders flow, team members pointed out that eight tickets in total were blocked due to missing information from the product-management team.

Surprisingly, the product manager did not appreciate the transparency. On the contrary, instead of acknowledging the indicated problems, he started to justify his own behaviour as well as the behaviour of his team members. In his point of view, they were not responsible for delivering the requested data.

Even in the smaller group meeting that followed the team stand-up, he showed no signs of insight but blamed the service team for being ineffective. As it turned out, the product manager rejected the basic idea that working less is the only way to achieve more and increase the quality of both product and decisions. "Nonsense," he said, and insisted that changing demands from the customer only temporarily overwhelmed his team. I leave it to you to decide whether his resistance was due more to my bad explanation of WIP limits or to the fact that these limits are both provocative and counterintuitive for most managers.

If you put design in process, you need the workers and managers to have a common means of understanding how the work works. This language and understanding is built as they learn together how and how well their organization works – as a system. (Seddon 2008, p.78)

In the title of *Learning to See* (Rother and Shook 2003), Mike Rother and John Shook point out the motto for this process of building common ground. As I show in the next chapter, we need to design proper meeting formats and provide professional facilitation to find out what the design of our system should look like. Yet learning to see how you work together to make your work does not necessarily mean that managers encourage self-organisation. The current management system may still build on one-way communication and centralised control. Chances are, you discover mistrust and misunderstanding rather than common ground. It could even become obvious that managers behave dysfunctionally.

Introducing Scrum and Kanban guarantees neither that the whole system will improve automatically nor that dysfunctional management behaviour will change just like that. Even the best visual work-management system will basically mirror the current leadership culture. As I outline in more detail in the chapter on changing, systemic improvement needs more than seeing. It needs a culture of feedback loops to highlight blind spots and the ability to hold each other accountable across functional or hierarchical boundaries.

Do you need an example to illustrate what this can look like in practice?

Improvement is not a given

In 2013, I was involved with the IT department of a German aircraft supplier where the team lead impeded self-organisation in many ways, apparently without noticing it.

Although a visual work-management system was in place, the team lead himself designed it and then pushed it onto the team. Driven by his best intentions to provide the right solution, he neither helped the team to understand why the system had to change nor how this change was supposed to be managed. Above all, stand-ups took the form of status reports and task allocation by the team lead. No wonder that nothing really changed for the better.

The story in the box emphasises the risk that managers remain command-and-control-aholics, using exchange and learning as an excuse for on-going micro-management. Design-wise, the story of the aircraft supplier reminded me of one of my favourite cartoons, shown in figure 20. As a matter of fact, effective management in a self-organising environment needs a tricky balance between designing the container and giving freedom, setting the stage and observing the play, stepping in and holding back. Swinging too far in either direction hampers team learning as Esther Derby argues.

Helicopter managers step in too soon. They swoop in at the first whiff of a problem to "rescue" the team. They deprive the team of the chance to think, solve problems, and decide together. These managers may believe they are doing the team a favour; what they really do is hamper the team development.

Absentee managers throw up their hands and say "you figure it out", no matter what the issue, or whether the team has the skill and authority to solve the problem. These mangers let the team flail and churn, wasting time and building frustration. People do learn from mistakes; but when people feel frustrated, hopeless or abandoned by their manager, increased capability is not the likely learning outcome. (Derby 2009)

Figure 20: Organisation design for effective collaboration.

Even though these categories may be too polarising, I saw similar things in the IT department of the aircraft supplier mentioned above. When one of the senior managers called me in to help with another change initiative that encompassed the kanban system, I struggled to find the right balance between respecting and confronting the manager. Does "start with what you do now" mean I had to respect his current behaviour even though it was obviously hindering self-organisation? Should I overlook how the team lead hijacked stand-ups? Even more importantly, how could I be of any help given that there was no explicit request to do so?

Experiments in redesigning the management role

What helped me to finally overcome my dilemma was an accident. It was deep winter and streets were blocked by tons of snow, and this team lead could not make it to a retrospective on time. Usually, he always facilitated the retrospectives but he called me and asked me to step into his role. You may call it another accident that I didn't follow the team lead's proposed approach, which focused on the well-known questions "What has gone well since the last retrospective?", "What hasn't?", and "What impedes our work?" Although I suspected that he wanted me to facilitate a call-out of the individual answers, I didn't do that either.

Instead, I started with a round of appreciative inquiry (see page 113). I asked the team to split up into pairs and conduct interviews focusing on three simple questions: "What has been a highlight for you, working on this team so far?"; "Without being too humble, what personal strengths can you build on?"; "What helps you to apply your strengths and what hinders you?" I invited them to conduct two rounds of interviews, each about 15 minutes long, exclusively focused on listening and taking notes, and asked them to summarise their most important insights on all three questions on sticky notes. You can probably imagine what they came up with in the presentation. Since I was fortunate to be trusted enough, the team used this opportunity to vent a mixture of disappointment, puzzlement, and anger. To most of them, it was crystal clear that the biggest impediment to using their individual strengths and realise their potential as a team was the relationship between them and their team lead. And they expressed some fear of confronting him with their negative feelings and their wish for more freedom and trust. I asked them if they wanted me to step up and act as a kind of a messenger, although I know what usually happens to messengers. They were relieved and gave me the mandate to use the sticky-note board they had created out of their interviews.

Surprisingly, the team lead was neither shocked nor embarrassed when confronted with the results of the team's retrospective. It was more a relief for him because he had somehow felt the same way. Building on this unexpected openness, I invited him to do what I've done quite often since then: to rethink leadership from the customer's point of view. Rather than "repair" both roles and relationships and risk curing only symptoms, I asked him to review what was actually needed in terms of leadership if the focus was on doing whatever has to be done to fulfil if not exceed the customer's expectations. The C/D/E model I used to better explain my idea resonated quite positively with the team lead and encouraged a radical review of the "what" and "how" of management and team work. We started to define value-oriented categories of service rather than an infinite flow of tasks to be done in daily business. Table 2 represents some results of our joint discovery process.

Service	How this adds value	Cust	Team	Org
Clarify product strategy	Helps to focus all efforts	x	x	x
Engage the customer	Direct communication to learn as early as possible	x	x	
Facilitate meetings	Empower team leads to manage themselves		x	
Align with other teams	Focus on end-to-end value streams and seek synergies		x	x

Table 2: Results of review with team lead.

In Switzerland, I was involved in a similar experiment to redesign the management role (see Kaltenecker and Beyer 2014). In this case, the experiment was kicked off by the manager of an IT-infrastructure department and driven by some sense of urgency, since the department manager was planning to take a four-month sabbatical. Hence, some handovers were inevitable. Working quite successfully with kanban for a long period of time, the department manager knew about the benefits of making things as visible and explicit as possible. That's why he decided to challenge his daily business by raising some rather radical questions. How do I actually create value as a manager? How do I contribute to fulfil our customer expectations? How do I support my teams, help my management peers, and address other stakeholders' interests throughout the organisation? If there were something like leadership work types, what would they look like?

Once the department manager defined his service catalogue of specific responsibilities that encompassed many different activities (see figure 21), it was clear how to use them. After a feedback loop with his team leads, checking everybody's understanding and possible gaps, the leadership team agreed on a clear process for handing over the services. This process consisted of the following steps:

- finally asking the business-unit manager for feedback on the catalogue;
- reviewing the services and aligning different expectations;
- defining what to hand over to whom;
- defining the collaboration between the respective services;
- kicking off the new leadership structure; and
- communicating responsibilities and interfaces to both the teams and the stakeholders.

Figure 21: Part of the management-services catalogue.

By the way, the experiment was considered very successful. The teams felt no particular deficits, stakeholders were happy, the team leads felt empowered, and the department manager enjoyed his sabbatical. The experiment was so successful that on his return, the department manager did not take back most of the management services as planned. Instead, he used some slack time to focus on the broader level of changing in the whole business unit.

One more example should emphasise that redesigning the management role is not just the business of individual managers.

Recently, I was involved with the management team of an Austrian engineering department. Similar to the Swiss department manager, the head of engineering made an explicit decision to focus on leadership. As all their implementation teams were working with Scrum and/or

Kanban, everybody on the management team was familiar with lean and agile thinking. Although the teams had successfully adopted the new methods, the managers observed an obvious downside. "Everybody feels like leading the whole department," one of the managers summarised. There was widespread confusion around roles and responsibilities. No wonder, as we identified six different roles that were supposed to lead in some way.

Because of this, the head of engineering decided to run a workshop on leadership design. Preparing for the workshop I was invited to facilitate, we agreed on some guiding questions. What is the current situation like? What works? Where do we see room for improvement? What kind of leadership is actually needed to fulfil our customer's expectations? What are key services that add value to our work process? Who should be responsible for what?

Starting with a retrospective, we examined what the department was doing and how that contributed to the current problems. Afterwards, we changed perspective by looking for the demand for leadership in the first place. Step by step, we worked our way from demand to capabilities, activities, roles, and alignments. After confronting the complexity of leadership in a lean and agile environment, we managed to simplify it in a consistent manner. Using various forms of visual management, we boiled down the initial picture to a reasonable number of services.

As shown in table 2, we even managed to map these services to existing roles.

Leadership Service	Activities	PO	TL	Te
Build Strategy	Clarify context & big picture Give direction – define the vision & set compelling goals Provide transparency and clarity in regard with roles, expectations and boundaries Deliver context – alignment, understanding, direction			

Leadership Service	Activities	PO	TL	Te
Create a lean, lightweight structure	Focus on customer-oriented value streams Design an organisation with as little handovers and dependencies as possible Allow for loose coupling of organisational units			
Empower people	Give freedom & improve capability Professionally facilitate all processes Remove impediments to encourage faster delivery Clarify responsibility and decision-making authorities			
Engage our customers	Reduce the distance between the teams and their customer Implement discovery phase, encourage user tests Involve the customer to provide better answers to their needs Build great/cool products – understand needs & provide value-add			

Table 3: Cut-out of leadership services, activities, roles, and responsibilities.

The management team also agreed on a clear strategy for reviewing and communicating the new setup. Again, a functional system for fast feedback loops with key players, peers from other business units, and senior management was crucial for the ultimate success of the effort.

Some conclusions

What is the moral of the stories? Once again, I think it was important to start the respective experiments with what the managers had done so far. I don't see any sense in confronting them with a predefined design for their role. On the one hand, it is a matter of general respect; on the other hand, it always pays to go with the current flow and use what works to address what does not. Although it was rather coincidental in the case of the aircraft supplier, I have met many managers since then, such as the infrastructure department lead or engineering managers, who were willing to redesign their roles if they see their own needs recognised as well.

To review leadership in service categories makes as much sense as the explicit focus on value rather than task. First and foremost, it helps to set the right boundaries for leadership as a team sport. It starts with the setup. Who should be on the team? What mixture of knowledge, skills, and experience do we actually need? How do the selected people fit together? Building on the soccer analogy outlined in the "What is leading self-organising teams all about?" chapter, we have to know how to score and how to prevent our opponents from doing so. Hence, managers have to take care that their teams do not consist only of strikers or midfielders. They need a good blend of capabilities so that all contribute to the overall success. They need proper training. And they need the right means to communicate and align with each other, internally but also across the set boundaries.

Reviewing the C/D/E model introduced in the "What are self-organising teams?" chapter, we could define five specific management services for effective contextual support of self-organisation:

- **setting the boundaries to** clarify the general mission and specific goals of the team, to determine team composition, for decision-making policies, and for the expected feedback from metrics and meetings;
- **providing the right infrastructure,** in terms of the necessary technical equipment, a room big enough for all team members to occupy with appropriate physical space for everyone, open space to gather in, a creative environment, a good espresso machine, and the like;
- designing a proper **flow of information** that ensures transparency and provides all data that the teams need to competently execute

their work and the relevant data needed to regularly inform the most important stakeholders;

- **providing opportunities for education such as** focusing on consistent development rather than singular events, continuously bridging the notorious knowing-doing gap with subject-matter training, peer approaches, team building, internal mentoring, external coaching, and the like; and

- defining a **reward** system that guarantees economic as well as symbolic consequences for good team performance and business success.

All in all, this means macro-management instead of micro-management. Managers need to be designers rather than administrators in order to create value for their teams as well as for their customers. As we know, creating value also takes some creativity, including the famous "creative destruction" necessary for both economic innovation and social change. For line managers, this creativity is as much about overcoming any bureaucratic mind-set as it is about improving their own behaviours. Last but not least, it is also about constructively challenging the team, building on the privileged position of informed outsider, close enough to but never part of the team. This position challenges at least two cornerstones of the traditional management role. First, the authority of managers is not based on being able to do their job better but on their ability to help others do their own jobs better by developing their skills and connecting with the rest of the organisation in order to provide a supportive context for the teams. Second, the manager's responsibilities no longer need a heroic mind-set.

Whereas the heroic manager of the past knew all, could do all and could solve every problem, the post-heroic manager asks how every problem can be solved in a way that develops other people's capacity to handle it. It is not virtuous to do it this way, it is essential. These organizations do not work if it is left to one person. Everyone has to be capable or nothing happens. (Handy 2002, p.132)

Far away from re-introducing control, this post-heroic mind-set encourages the manager to intensively observe the team's interactions and provide professional feedback. The manager can review the team's results, appreciate their strengths, and challenge their weaknesses. In my point of view, the manager's role is not only about being the distant supporter or nice gardener, it is essentially about being an active sparring partner who is courageous enough to shed light on potential blind spots and helps the team to improve for the sake of the customer. Systemically thinking, managers can act as catalysts that provoke a higher order of self-organisation at the team level as well as the enterprise level – and improve themselves by meeting the challenges and building on the hints they receive from their teams.

Because these process improvements should not be separated from daily business, establishing a system of action-oriented feedback loops is key to any improvement. The guidelines for designing your action review cycle (page 108) should provide a better understanding of what this system could look like. Given that it is professionally facilitated as a regular cycle, it could be an essential driver of what Henrik Kniberg (2011, p.53) calls the "process improvement engine", powered by a simple formula:

- clarity (we know what is going on);
- communications (we talk openly about positive and negative things); and
- data (we learn from personal feedback as well as from systemic metrics).

Certainly, this cannot be done all at once. As is true for self-organising teams, becoming a post-heroic manager does not happen overnight. That's why I have also good experience with helping managers to pursue small, time-boxed experiments rather than big change initiatives, which threaten most people. These small experiments – like rotating the responsibility for facilitating, merging redundant meetings, giving up traditional status reporting, or restraining from individual job assignments – usually pay off for both managers and teams. Have a look at the guidelines on page 107 for reviewing and redesigning your management role.

Why do we take yet another round of evolutionary approach instead of the management revolution supported by some scholars? Why change a highly dysfunctional circumstance in small steps rather than blow it away with revolutionary spirit? Why not just kick off the new generation of management by design? My simple-minded answer is that we should not forget that **redesigning your role as a line manager** does not mean that you cognitively understand the current challenges. More than that, changing management focus and design is also an emotional journey. To exploit the power of self-organising systems in an agile environment, the manager must be willing to give up "some of the psychic satisfactions of being a command-and-control manager: the thrill of exercising power and telling other people what to do, of being seen, to be in charge, of living out tiny Napoleon dreams of power, of being someone who can make an arbitrary decision just for the heck of it." (Denning 2010, p.112)

To design for macro-management rather than micro-management seems to be a good starting point for this journey. This doesn't mean line managers are superfluous in a lean and agile environment. On the contrary, it means focusing on the enabling conditions on a systems level and making sure that you are doing the best you can to support self-organising processes. It also means avoiding the tendency to micro-manage tasks whenever you feel nervous or uncertain about whether the team will achieve its goals. This resonates with Steven Spear's change requests for a management system that is able to address the challenges of the 21st century.

(Managers) are not in place to command, control, berate, intimidate, or evaluate through a contrived set of metrics, but to ensure that their organizations become even more self-diagnosing and self-improving, skilled at detecting problems, solving them and multiplying the effect by making the solutions available throughout the organization. (Spear 2009, p.26)

Facilitating

In his popular business fable *The Five Dysfunctions of a Team* (2002), Patrick Lencioni highlights five key challenges for each group to master:

- Build trust.
- Manage the fear of conflict by clarifying differences of all sorts.
- Get honest commitment to the overall mission and specific goals of the group.
- Hold each other accountable in a respectful and consistent manner.
- Focus on results by delivering real value for the customer.

What do all these challenges have in common? Well, they need professional facilitation to be met. Upon a closer look, I can identify three formats in which facilitation takes place in a self-organising environment: one-on-one dialogues, whether informal chats around the water cooler (in Austria, around the coffee machine) or in more formal conversations such as peer coaching, performance feedback, or mentoring; group conversations in meetings; and large-group events that are good for getting to know more colleagues, sharing knowledge across boundaries, and aligning the perspectives of multiple stakeholders or other development purposes.

In line with Lencioni, I want to assert that for all these formats, trust building is essential. Far more than touchy-feely stuff, trust is essential for the quality of all interactions. Using a mechanistic metaphor, one could say that it is the oil that keeps the social machine running. Trust does not only feel good and motivate people, it also catalyses the team's rational commitment to the work as well as the emotional commitment to each other. Lean and agile methods facilitate commitment by encouraging teams to manage their own work, pull from prioritised work lists or "done" columns, and focus on continuously improving their work practices. These trust-based practices are at the heart of self-organisation and are the driving force for achieving good results as a team.

The Role of a Leader

The Five Dysfunctions of a Team

Figure 22: Lencioni's dysfunctions model.

But how can you build trust? What can you do to create the foundation of your teamwork? Trust building is not limited to fancy team workshops or other social events outside your daily business. On the contrary, trust building happens all the time at all levels – or not. However, you can deliberately use some facilitation techniques to support it. The easiest way to start is with one-on-one dialogues

Facilitating one-on-one dialogues

I'd like to recommend two specific practices that have proven to be helpful in various situations: appreciative inquiry and humble inquiry. Both practices have a lot in common:

- Both are devoted to learning more about each other and the situation at hand.
- Both work in one-on-one setups and help to ignite group conversations.
- Both allow you to share deeper insights.
- Both serve as a catalyst for meta-level conversations such as: "What does our big picture look like?"; "What are the most interesting commonalities and differences you can identify?"; "What main

themes meander through the different stories?"; "What does it tell you about this group?"; "What would a colleague from team XYZ think of your situation?"

- Both use two simple techniques for this purpose: questions and active listening.

Tables 3 and 4 remind you what these classic communication techniques are about.

Questions	How?	Why?
Open	Who? How? When? What? Where? Which?	To get information and show respect.
Closed	Questions aimed at getting a "Yes" or "No".	To clarify facts and focus on decision making
Scaling	How much? E.g. on a continuum from 1 to 10? Defined by %?	To estimate connections and clarify urgencies.
Circular	What does X think of the situation? How could our customer see this?	To discover different perspectives and explore assumptions.

Table 3: Types of questions.

Listening	How?	Why?
Body language	Open attitude, eye contact, nodding, social grunting (hmm...).	To send positive impulses and show the right mind-set.
Paraphrasing	Repeat what you have heard in your own words.	To pay attention and check your understanding.
Acknowledging emotions	E.g. "It seems you are embarrassed about...".	To allow for emotions and apply empathy.
Summarising	Distil your conversation.	To define core results.

Table 4: Criteria for active listening.

Neither appreciative nor humble inquiry is driven by tools though. They aren t checklists to follow or a simple set of prewritten questions. They are behaviours that come out of respect and are based on real interest and individual curiosity. If you think you know everything up front, why ask about it? Questions show respect because questioning means admitting your ignorance in the respective area. Besides, questions put the other person in a position of authority. The responder has the answer and you are kindly asking him or her to share knowledge and insight.

At the heart of the initial approach (see Cooperrider and Whitney 2005), appreciative inquiry serves as a catalyst for getting to know each other better by exploring a specific subject or knowledge. For instance, you can focus on leadership experience and combine this with personal information about highlights, challenges, and strengths. To create as much safety as possible, use a worksheet with a few questions and space for notes (see page 113 for a sample). I recommend the interview format because each participant is supposed to pay full attention to the other for a predetermined length of time (usually 10 to 15 minutes). Then the partners change sides. Besides the obvious benefit of helping us to learn, appreciative inquiry is an easy way to become familiar with dialoguing, often without even noticing it. Unlike a discussion with its usual ingredients of long arguments, interruptions, and speaking before thinking, dialogue is based on listening and reflection (see table 5).

Dialogue	Discussion
Starts with listening.	Starts with speaking.
Is about speaking with.	Is about speaking to.
Focuses on insights.	Focuses on differences.
Is collaborative.	Is competitive.
Encourages reflection.	Encourages quick thinking.

Table 5: Dialogue versus discussion.

Based on the work of physicist David Bohm, William Isaacs (1999), director of the MIT Dialogue Project, defines four core dialoguing skills:

- voicing what you truly think and feel, expressing your ideas as well as your emotions;
- listening and opening up to deeply understand what is being expressed, focusing on your partner and asking questions for clarification;
- respecting and acknowledging the inevitable differences between your partner and you, and exercising curiosity to find out as much as possible about these differences while excluding the usual judgments of better/faster/higher etc.; and
- suspending your own opinions and actively questioning your beliefs and assumptions.

I especially like the flexibility of appreciative inquiry in a dialogue: you can tailor your focus and select different questions. Last but not least, you can decide how much the interview partners share with the whole group. An easy way to share is by letting the partners distil their most interesting insights. You can invite them to write these insights on sticky notes and present them to the larger group (see figure 23).

Alternatively, you can facilitate a call-out. If you want to add some extra flavour, ask the partners to summarise separately and then to introduce each other without further discussion – this guarantees some surprises, mostly funny ones.

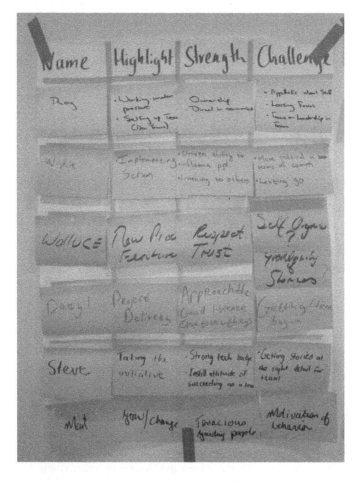

Figure 23: Keywords on appreciative inquiries.

I use appreciative inquiry for multiple purposes: to kick off a team-building event, to start stakeholder workshops, to challenge leadership trainees, and as an alternative way to gather data in retrospectives.

Whereas appreciative inquiry is based on learning by storytelling, humble inquiry follows a different path. On the one hand, the purpose is more diagnostic in terms of exploring causes, motives, feelings, and systemic patterns (see the sample list of questions on page 114). On the other hand, it is more dynamic and should to be applied in a process-oriented manner with respect to the situation: "What kind of information do we need to make a good decision?"; "What is missing to really understand the current problem in order to create the right solution?"; "What do we think will happen if we shift our focus?"

Certainly, these questions are not limited to one-on-one conversations. On the contrary, as I show in the next section, they are powerful tools for facilitating group conversations, too.

Facilitating group conversations

I remember more than one team situation where it helped to pay attention to causes and systems rather than symptoms and individual actions. "When in doubt take it to the team" is old yet good advice for any self-organising environment. Humbly involve everybody in your fact-finding mission and give all team members the chance to speak up, for instance by facilitating a so-called go-around, which is a simple yet effective means to gather diverse data before jumping to conclusions and actions (see guidelines on page 115).

Certainly, it does not hurt to have a prewritten worksheet to prepare you for solution-oriented questions, let alone how to handle the answers you get. However, these questions are even more powerful if you use them in specific situations in which you have no clue what is really going on.

Once, I facilitated the retrospective of a Scrum team that was struggling to deliver the stories the members had committed to. As expected of this classic problem of teams relatively new to Scrum, the usual suspects showed up in a root-cause analysis: overestimating capability, being pushed to overcommit by an ambitious product owner, and not measuring real progress. Consequently, effective countermeasures were discussed, clarified, and agreed on.

Yet the next retrospective revealed that nothing had really happened, let alone improved. Again, the team had failed to deliver. During review of what had happened, Marlene, a senior developer, burst out in frustration:

"We'll never deliver something! We are simply too stupid!" Some of her colleagues slowly nodded while others looked down. Everybody fell silent for a long time that almost felt like eternity to me. I wondered what I should do? Ask Marlene for further clarification? Help to calm her? Continue the retrospective as planned? Take a break?

While trying to clear my mind, Carl, a junior on the team, spoke up. "I think you hit the nail on the head, Marlene. Let's start talking about how we feel about our constant failure! What is going on?" In this way, Carl invited the team to humbly inquire into their situation apart from purely intellectual reflection. More and more, the team members started to talk about their emotions: their disappointment and frustration but also their true aspirations to show what they felt they were actually able to do.

Back on track as facilitator, I did my best to help them master this uncomfortable process. Going with the emotional flow, I made sure that everybody could purge himself or herself before others interrupted or started to discuss different issues. At the end, I summarised what has been said and made a few notes on a flip chart. As it turned out, there was a substantial level of distrust on the team. Hidden conflicts popped up. Two team members had had a bad experience with each other. Another was frustrated because he was supposed to move to another team. Mindfully, the team inquired into the underlying biases and false assumptions that led to lack of commitment and the inability to hold each other accountable. They agreed to hold one-on-one conversations to further clarify relationships and re-establish as much trust as possible. As you can imagine, the next sprint was quite successful and the retrospective a celebration of positive conflict management.

To me, there were two morals to be learned. First, humble inquiry is not a privilege of a dedicated facilitator; everybody is entitled to ask the right questions to bring a team forward. Second, if you feel confused as a facilitator and you feel like you cannot help the group anymore, try embracing your uncertainty rather than ignoring it. Don't expect yourself to be confident and ahead of the group dynamics all of the time. Acknowledge the limits of your knowledge and give yourself time to think. Trust the team to come up with the next step. This is what self-organising is about.

Once the conversation starts again, you can post summarised statements on a flip chart or even invite the team to split up in pairs or trios to create smaller and therefore safer containers for addressing potentially hot topics. By going first in managing your own fears, however, you also encourage people to express what they really care about, thus helping the whole group to overcome the fear of exploring potential conflicts.

That's exactly why I see humble inquiry as a key leadership practice – again, mirroring one of the core values of leading self-organising teams, to be understood as a behaviour that comes out of respect. By helping people to express their authentic ideas, feelings, and questions, chances are good that you prevent further escalation of fear and the resistance that often comes along with it.

If in doubt, you can always facilitate a go-around as mentioned above. Grant everybody a length of time for an uninterrupted statement, mindfully visualise a summary of these statements, look at the list of collected statements, and start another round of review. What did we learn so far? What has become clearer? How does that affect our further actions? For visualisation, especially in a process-oriented manner, it might be helpful to keep some professional guidelines for chart writing in mind (see page 116).

Meeting management in a self-organising environment

Successfully facilitating group conversations needs more than some smart questions. According to the C/D/E model, we should build the right container for supporting open exchanges. In other words, you have to create the right conditions under which people can best collaborate. In the lean and agile world, we have at least three classic formats for group conversations: stand-ups, reviews, and retrospectives. Today, both the purpose and the structure seem to be common sense: operational coordination in a short stand-up (see guidelines on page 117); show your customers and other stakeholders what you've achieved and get feedback in the product review (see guidelines on page 118); present data on your performance, explain how your customers and other stakeholders benefit, and explore what you could improve in the operations review (see page 119); and reflect on the work process and how to improve collaboration in the retrospective. Various practitioners provide valuable ideas on how to facilitate these classic meetings: Jason Yip (2011) on stand-ups, Peter Hundermark (2014) and David Anderson (2010) on reviews, and Esther

Derby and Diana Larsen (2006) and Luis Gonçalves and Ben Linders (2014) on retrospectives.

What do these conversations have in common? What's behind the different formats? And what can we learn from these formats for facilitating any other meeting? "Meetings are as common as dirt and about as popular," Marvin Weisbord and Sandra Janoff (2007) point out in their landmark book on facilitation, *Don't Just Do Something, Stand There!* They offer clear principles for leading meetings that matter:

- **Manage structure**, the conditions under which people interact, not behaviour. Start each facilitation process from the outside in. What is the purpose of the meeting? What specific goals do you pursue? Have you got the right people to achieve the goals? Do you have enough time, enough people, and enough group maturity?

- **Match participants to goals**. Invite people to share responsibility, and pay attention to the use of space and time. In C/D/E language: control a meetingou got the r and ensure a good mixture of perspectives, and participants usually will take care of all the exchanges necessary to achieve the set goals.

- **Give people time to express themselves**. Let them collect their thoughts and differentiate their stakes, help them with the right methods to generate joint insights, and facilitate action-oriented decisions.

- **Encourage self-management**. Suggest that people take roles as recorders, reporters, timekeepers, or local facilitators, and interfere as little as possible. Give them the freedom to find their own way to accomplish the expected outcome.

- **Talk less and pay attention more**. Observe and listen. Apply appreciative or humble inquiry, encourage open exchange, provide feedback if necessary, and invite people to say what is on their minds without prompting them to behave according to your plan.

- **Work with people the way they are**, not as you wish them to be. Whether or not you explicitly refer to the popular "Prime Directive" (see the preface), assume that everybody is doing the best they can.

- **Pay attention to yourself**. Be aware of your agitation, your fear that things are getting out of hand, and your impulse to fix it fast. "The more we learn to live with uncertainty and remain curious about what's to come, the better prepared we are to value each group's struggle."

- Applying these principles allows us to turn any meeting into a laboratory for self-organisation. Rather than waste time with boring reports or sit together with the wrong people in a bad setup, we can empower our meetings by creating the right boundaries within which the right people can jointly focus on the right things. No doubt, these principles are more easily stated than consistently implemented. Especially, the balance between paying attention to the topic, to the people, and to yourself as a facilitator remains a tricky one. Besides, there are a lot of potential challenges: drifting off topic, running out of time, dealing with dominant people, confronting unexpected team conflicts, handling lack of energy, and experiencing long moments of uncomfortable silence.

Moments of silence

What can professional facilitators do when they have actually no idea how to proceed? Weisbord and Janoff provide a simple recipe:

Don't do something only for the sake of it: stand there and contain your feelings.

Be aware of your agitation, your fear that things are getting out of hand, and your impulse to fix it quickly.

Wait, look around, and make eye contact with as many participants as possible.

Exhale as much as you can.

Take a big, deep breath.

Hold it a few seconds, e.g. by slowly counting to 10.

Repeat as needed until somebody says what needs saying.

The above recipe has helped me in various crises. Most of the times that I have held back without losing contact, someone on the team finally started to talk. Surprisingly, in most cases, nobody except me showed any signs of uncertainty and stress. On the contrary, often people simply needed some time to think or take a break before they could engage in more meaningful action.

The more we learn to live with uncertainty and remain curious about what's to come, the better prepared we are to value each group's struggle. So we resist the tendency to manage our own anxiety by talking, asking questions, explaining, repeating, or changing the subject. When we're not sure what to do, we don't do anything. (Weisbord and Janoff 2007, p.132)

Large-group facilitation

- If you're still keen to apply your facilitation capabilities, I have one more challenge to offer: the format of large-group events. What are large-group events? Why do we need them? How do we facilitate them? Large groups include more than 20 people. With groups this size, it's no longer possible to interact with a team-based mind-set. It's hard to keep an overview on what is going on because there is usually an overwhelming amount of local action. As a facilitator, you're dealing with organisational rather than team dynamics.

Why bother with large groups when your focus is on leading self-organising teams? As argued in the introductory chapters, self-organising teams are not lonesome islands. There is a sea of organisational dynamics around them, setting their context, determining their boundaries, and thereby highly influencing how self-organisation can take place. Think of a mission that might change due to new customer demands, of the need to redesign your container due to new dependencies with other teams, of changes in team composition, or of what all these contextual changes mean for the exchanges inside your team as well as with your stakeholders.

In short, you can use large group events to clarify the context of your self-organising team. When you are focused on improving systems rather than individuals, you need good practices for effective facilitation beyond the team level, bringing large-group facilitation skills into play. Professionally conducted, large-group events help us to:

- bring the right people together on a broader organisational level, e.g. for clarifying strategic topics, driving product innovation, or designing organisational change;
- focus a large group of diverse members on a common purpose, e.g. by focusing on strategic decisions (Where to go?), agreeing on product development (What to deliver to whom?), or aligning your different expectations (How to collaborate with each other?);

- work on the whole system and increase its self-organising capabilities, e.g. by openly exchanging information, intensively discussing your different points of view on important topics, sharing your knowledge and expertise, or facilitating a joint retrospective;

- engage head, heart, and spirit of everybody involved, e.g. by shaping an empowering container with the right mixture of participants, using interactive methods, or creating new opportunities for exchange;

- co-create new solutions, e.g. by designing a system for continuous improvement or focusing on cross-departmental blocks and constraints; and

- collectively commit to compelling action, e.g. by updating your change board, deciding on what are most important improvements, or having a clear action plan.

"Exploring the whole elephant" may be the motto for this type of event. As for any other meeting, large-group events need a clear focus and an agenda defined by expected outcomes (see the checklist for large-group events on page 121). Since you have to facilitate a lot of parallel interactions, you need to even more thoroughly prepare and plan your design. Since setting the right boundaries is even more important, facilitating a large-group event often starts with the logistics. Secure the right venue for the expected number of participants: a large central room with breakout rooms for smaller sessions and proper infrastructure.

Even the layout of the room plays an important role. Figure 24 shows the plan for the Scrum Clinic, a large event that took place during the 2010 Scrum Gathering in Amsterdam. To provide expertise and guidance to participants, we created an open space in which we addressed hot topics in three sessions of 50 minutes, each run in 10 parallel groups and facilitated by two Certified Scrum Coaches. After each session, each group was expected to provide a written summary for display in a gallery in the break room. The event kicked off with a short, general introduction on the stage (see right side of the figure) and featured a marketplace (on the left) with all the necessary information regarding what, where, when, and facilitated by whom. Since we did not have enough breakout rooms, we decided to hold six sessions in the big room. Figure 25 shows what (part of) the room layout looked like in reality. Once you have clarified the boundaries, you can focus on the process of facilitating a large group to achieve a valuable outcome. What does the right flow look like? What information is needed prior to the event? How to set the stage for the event? What are the right ideas for exchanging information and generating insights? When to split up in small groups? When to align one another in the plenary? How to ensure that the right decisions are made? The guidelines for facilitating large-group events on page 121 should help you to keep overview and find proper answers to these questions.

Figure 24: Planned layout for the Scrum Clinic.

Figure 25: What the Scrum Clinic actually looked like.

Some conclusions

However, facilitating a large group event is also a good opportunity to learn more about what it means to lead in a self-organising environment. On the one hand, you need all the core capabilities defined in this workbook: a clear focus to create value for all participants, a design that encourages goal-oriented flow, the right facilitation skills to guide the process, and the ability to inspect and adapt according to what's actually happening. On the other hand, one of your biggest challenges is to effectively align multiple self-organising processes. In most cases, these processes happen in so-called table groups, small teams of six to eight members consisting of the right mixture of people who self-organise themselves within the set boundaries of different work assignments. In order to make the most of your gathering, you can remix these table groups to create new differences and encourage even more exchange across different areas of expertise, levels of hierarchy, or business locations.

But you also need to think about how to align these groups to go beyond the local interactions and distil organisational insights. Therefore you can ask the group to choose a speaker to present its most important results, have a transparent Q & A with a podium of selected people, or send delegates to a fish bowl (a small circle in the middle of a larger ring) to encourage a more intense discussion of results, usually including an open "hot chair" to encourage spontaneous input from the outer circle. There are many ways to distil joint insights while experiencing the complexity of organisational alignment and decision making.

Finally, I would like to mention one more dimension of self-organising: the facilitator team you need to manage all these things, from the preparation for the event to the professional documentation to the debriefing. Bring the right mixture of skilled people together, clarify your mission with your sponsor, and enjoy the power of yet another self-organising unit.

Today, there are a lot of methods for large-group interventions. There are the classic two to three-day conference formats such as real-time strategic change or future search, with a clear flow of events. We have smaller, more flexible formats such as world café (see the guidelines on page 123) or open space (see page 124). Finally, we have solo design elements that can you can easily scale and tailor to your specific situations. For instance, you can also use appreciative inquiry (see page 113) with more than 100 people – it's best to set up table groups of six to eight participants. Focus the core actions (interviews, presentation, and review) on the table groups, finally scaling the information and feedback loops by asking each group to elect a speaker to present the most important commonalities and differences of that table to the room. You can have a large session of lean coffee (see the guidelines on page 125) either with more than one circle or with each circle focusing on one specific topic, with a final presentation of each circle's most interesting outcome.

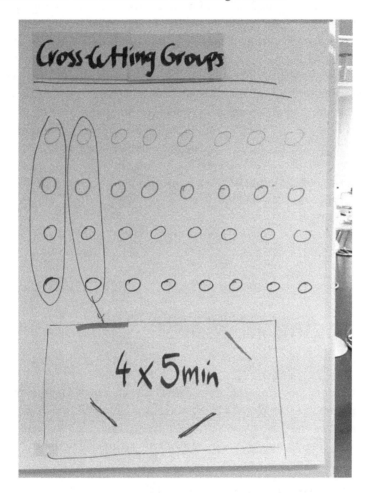

Figure 26: How to build crosscutting groups.

You can build crosscutting groups after a round of focus groups (see figure 26). Each crosscutting group consists of at least one member of each focus group. This way, you can encourage high-energy exchanges of dialogue within small groups over formal presentations in the plenary. If you have all focus groups visualise their most important results, you can combine crosscutting groups with a gallery walk, facilitating stand-ups in front of each visualisation. Finally, you may use the famous "law of the two feet" of open space whenever you facilitate different focus groups. This law encourages not only potentially innovative cross-pollination but also allows the freedom to self-organise around topics or to cut yourself some slack if needed.

All these elements build on forming new groups and encouraging new exchanges across the usual functional and hierarchical boundaries. They encourage self-organising processes beyond the given organisational containers. I'd like to encourage you to run your own experiments to find out more about how transparency and empowerment improve on what used to be done behind closed doors: change management, strategic development, knowledge exchange, silo bridging, and trust building to name a few. I'd also like to remind you to be mindful when preparing for the right container and creating your design. Start small, especially if you've never facilitated large-group events, and scale as needed. And don't do it alone! Gather at least a small group of helpers, best with a mix of expertise. Last but not least, enjoy being part of another self-organising team!

Changing

////////////////////////////

"For the times they are a-changing" Bob Dylan sang in 1964. Over the last 50 years, we've experienced a tremendous amount of change at all levels. As argued in the "What are self-organising teams?" chapter, change is no longer something you want to postpone as long as possible. Today, change is on everybody's menu.

What does that mean for leading self-organising teams? What kind of challenges can you expect and how can you effectively deal with them? As shown, self-organising systems are characterised by **continuous adaptation** to changing environments. They build on feedback in order to adjust to the challenges they face. Leadership takes place in all local interactions, from which structure emerges. Keeping these characteristics in mind, you can expect changes on three different levels:

Changes on the personal level may be motivated by the shock of unexpected challenges or the willingness to challenge yourself, by survival anxiety, or by your appetite to learn new patterns of behaviour.

Changing perspectives

I remember working with a cross-functional group of IT and business people on their meeting structure. While we started out quite energetically, we became more and more lost the deeper we dived into the topic. What meetings did the group actually need to have? How do we ensure that those meetings are valuable for all participants? And what do we do if a few people argue that the daily stand-up meeting is superfluous while others insist that this meeting is the most important to them?

As a facilitator, I was worrying what to do next. We seemed to be trapped in the classic dead-end street. I could feel the tension in the room as well as my own. Realising how rigid I felt and assuming that I was not the only one who felt that way, I decided to interrupt the process. "It feels like we are going nowhere," I heard myself say. "Let's start changing this situation with a simple first step." Encouraged by some curious faces, I stood up and invited them to do the same. This small postural change was immediately accompanied by some sighs as well as laughter. "Ready for an experiment to change perspectives?" I asked.

Many of them nodded while I tried to make eye contact with all eight of them. I could build on their trust in me as a facilitator. I asked them to relax by stretching and shaking their arms and legs, which caused another round of laughter and funny comments. Finally, I asked them to do two more things. First, I asked them to step behind their chairs and review their current point of view. What has been achieved so far? What would the next small improvement look like? Second, I asked them to select the chair of a colleague to stand behind and to reflect on that colleague's point of view for a minute. I was not aware that I was actually running another experiment in self-organisation before I thanked them for their willingness to experiment and encouraged them to pair up with one of their peers, find a good place to chat, and talk about what had crossed their minds over the last couple of minutes.

Changes on the team level can be caused by changes in the number of team members, negative feedback from the customer, impulses to change for the better, dysfunctional work processes, or more innovative ways to build products.

Changes on the organisational level may arise from shifting customer demand, new competitors, changes in regulations that challenge if not undermine the organisational mission, discovery of new business opportunities, compelling vision, or fresh ideas for customer services. These changes might create new constraints for self-organising teams, call for different cross-team interactions, or transfer power to self-organising teams.

Referring to the C/D/E model, we can distinguish between changes of the container (first change level), which create new boundaries for self-organisation, and changes in the container (levels two and three), which create differences and new patterns of exchange. What kind of leadership is needed to successfully manage these specific changes?

Changes on the personal level: postural, retrospective, and experiments

Let's begin with the basic unit of change: yourself. To focus on your own changing capability is always a good starting point. There is good news for those of you who want to make a difference: that makes a difference. Even if you have systemic changes in mind, you can start small, as Steven Spear (2009) suggests. His advice? Forget about detailed analysis and complicated action plans. Instead:

- Focus on a problem in your area of influence.
- Start a local experiment.
- Proceed with small footprints but long legs.
- Don't think too much, but do a lot.
- Make sure you are getting viable feedback on your experiment.
- Evaluate your feedback.
- Decide whether to continue your experiment or stop it and try something else (in lean start-up language: pivot or persevere).

- Don't delay your changing experiment until you have enough free time because you never will.

If this sounds too abstract, try postural changes. I have often been astonished how much difference a small adjustment of embodied behaviours can make. Stand up if sitting, get closer if far away, take a step back if too close, move if rigid, open a window, go outdoors to take a bio break.

What can one learn from the experience described in the box? As you can imagine, this experiment did not immediately solve all the group issues. Nevertheless, the postural changes, the pure acts of standing up, stretching, and moving helped them to overcome some obvious blockades. I felt reminded of a basic lesson in change dynamics: with the first small change you make, you will make a difference to the current situation, at least for yourself. Sometimes, it is just this: a small step that helps you to change your own perspective. Sometimes, this first step helps you to change the pattern of interaction, too. As we all know from popular lean and agile practices, it can make a lot of a difference to stand up, to stand closer together, to talk directly to someone, or to stop talking and start listening. If we have a sustainable pace in mind, recognising how tense you are is a good point at which to act. At that moment, you can recognise that you need to relax, which often starts with getting control of your breathing, relaxing your muscles, and slowing down. These are proven practices for tiny (or not so tiny) situations that call for non-dramatic change.

Certainly, these small adjustments are not enough to master all change that confronts you. Unfortunately, we tend to focus too much on what we can change and too little on what we should change. If you are not clear about how to make a difference that makes a difference for yourself and for the people next to you, run a personal retrospective.

Ask yourself questions such as "What am I currently happy with?", "What works well?", "What doesn't?" Review your answers and learn more about your current whereabouts. Have a look at the questionnaire provided on page 129, spend some time away from your job at a place you like, and visualise whatever comes to mind in regard with the core questions of your choice. For my own retrospective, I prefer to use small sticky notes for each answer because they allow for more flexibility in clustering (green sticky notes for positive, red ones for negative experiences), defining proper headlines (blue sticky notes), and distilling action points (yellow sticky notes). Figure 27 shows what such a retro can look like.

If you don't want to limit yourself to looking back, try one of Charles Handy's exercises for looking into the future (see page 130). Drawing your lifeline, writing your own obituary, and assuming what friends would say about your specific qualities and how you use them in your daily business are proven means to discover new perspectives apart from building on what you have learned in the past.

Figure 27: A personal retrospective.

Changes on the team level: feedback, kata, and improvement

As argued, there are some easy ways to start changing yourself, like postural changes, personal retrospectives, and small experiments in problem solving. But if you are still not sure where you should focus, use another simple recipe: asking for feedback.

Why feedback? Akio Toyoda provides a straightforward answer (in Liker and Convis 2012): "If we do not give people accurate feedback based on real behaviour, they are not growing and we are not respecting them." Therefore, asking for feedback basically means asking for help. It should be clear that we understand this quest as a sign of responsibility, not as a symptom of weakness. And it should be clear that we are shifting the focus of change from the individual to the team level.

In my opinion, the willingness to ask for help is vital for any self-organising team. As various studies on team sports show, the performance of a team is directly correlated with the degree to which members help each other. But what does it mean to help? Helping is a chameleon-like phenomenon. It can take many different forms such as assisting, advising, or teaching (to name only a few). Being really helpful, nevertheless, is not a given. Chances are good that even the best-intended support is not helpful at all. The saying goes: "Please, do not help. It's already hard enough!"

Sometimes people even feel embarrassed by the way we try to help them. Sometimes our help is superficially welcome but practically ignored. Sometimes we are frustrated because what we regard as our most brilliant feedback is hardly noticed while some of our most routine questions turn out to be the crucial interventions for our peers. This all underlines that helping is a complex phenomenon. It is always, as Ed Schein explains, a multi-layered social process, grounded in trustful relationships (Schein 2009a).

Two questions remain: whom to ask for feedback and how to make sure that you receive something that helps you with your change efforts? There are many HR tools available such as 360-degree feedback, performance appraisals, leadership assessments, and the like. But all these tools need substantial effort and tend to be rather formal. They are neither focused on your individual need for help nor on fostering continuous improvement. A hands-on alternative for your feedback strategy is the spousal test. In line with Robert Kegan and Lisa Laskow Lahey's *Immunity to Change* (2009), this test is focused on the following questions:

- What is the single thing you think is most important for me to get better at?
- What is the one big thing I should work on?
- Where would you like to see improvements?

It is called spousal test because you are supposed to ask these questions of your spouse, best friend, or a family member close to you. If you don t want to rely on a single point of view, create your own 360-degree feedback by asking more people around you. I have already recommended this easy technique to many leaders, even to whole teams. Usually, people discover substantial overlap between the answers they get from various "spouses", which helps in finally distilling your one big thing to improve on.

Figure 28: An expanded Johari window.

Asking for feedback is even more important in a self-organising environment since we all tend to overestimate our ability to change. As argued in the chapter on focusing, there is a widespread illusion of skill that leads us to overestimate our true capability for changing. The same holds true for feedback as a key driver of any change. How can we overcome this illusion? Picking up the analogy of managers and athletes, we could ask ourselves how an athlete improves. Certainly, the athlete would need more than abstract explanations of how to do something better. Although we know that there is nothing more practical than a good theory, theory is not enough. The athlete will focus on doing in order to make the supposed difference a new habit. She or he will repeatedly practice in order to alter her or his behaviour and build a new routine. At the same time, the athlete will know that she or he is unable to objectively assess her or his own performance to gauge improvement and what additional things need work. This is because the illusion of skill also encompasses our inability to perceive our own habits accurately. In other words, we cannot see through our own blind spots just like that.

The Johari window in figure 28 explains why we do not know what we do not know. We're simply not aware of certain things, which are unknown to us but known to others. We need feedback in order to expand our open/public area and counterbalance our self-perception with the perceptions of others. That's why our athlete will practice under the observation and guidance of an experienced coach. In sports, you need a coach in order to model the behaviours you need to successfully compete. Since training is about continuous improvement, the necessity of a coach will not go away. If no one observes you and provides feedback, there is a high risk that you train for the wrong things and end up internalising the wrong routines.

That's exactly what the improvement and the coaching kata of the Toyota way are about. Kata literally means "routine". Like in sports, anyone keen to improve needs to perform the expected behaviour over and over. By the same token, a person needs continuous feedback in terms of perceptions as well as metrics (as argued in the chapter on focusing). The Toyota way to lean leadership explores what to focus on when leading self-organising teams. It is driven by continuous self-development with the help of an experienced mentor or coach. Here is Toyota's selection of skills to improve on (Rother 2009):

- open-minded observation of the work of the organisation;
- active listening to hear what people are really saying;
- understanding the actual strengths and weaknesses of each person;
- defining problems and identifying the root causes;
- identifying countermeasures to the true root causes;
- translating plans into action with clear accountability;
- taking the time and energy to identify further opportunities for improvement;
- influencing people across the organisation (with no direct authority); and
- being able to teach others all of the above.

"A loop a day keeps the trouble away," we joked some years ago. As a matter of fact, successful change is always driven by professional feedback loops. We loop into the future by combining action and reflection, making communication a two-way street, sharpening our listening and observing skills, and last but not least by asking for and receiving personal feedback on our leadership skills.

Figure 29: The fitness recipe for leading self-organising teams.

In short, the only way to bridge the notorious knowing-doing gap is by establishing a system that allows for consistent training, applying what has been learned, and getting fast feedback from our colleagues. Lean and agile methods provide many good practices for this such as:

- pair approaches of any kind, building on XP's pair-programming routines;
- peer coaching where colleagues help each other to solve difficult issues;
- communities of practice for knowledge sharing by functional experts;
- individual mentoring by a more experienced subject experts;
- expert coaching on or near the job, either provided by an internal or an external coach; and

- self-organised training and coaching circles such as the local groups of the Scrum or LeanKanban communities for knowledge exchange and the practical application of new tools.

Changing how we learn from each other

Recently, the management team of a German IT services provider used feedback sheets in consecutive team-building events. Team members filled out and handed in the sheets in an open circle at the first event in May. A second event in November started with the team members receiving the same sheets they initially wrote six months earlier. All were asked to update their feedback with special focus on what had been improved since May.

This update, also openly exchanged within the group, fostered not only confidence in giving and receiving feedback. It encouraged the willingness to strengthen the feedback culture throughout the whole organisation. "This will definitely drive us forward," one of the managers enthusiastically summarised after they had agreed on using the same feedback sheets as a kind of a living document for quarterly updates.

Core teams should be encouraged to provide peer feedback as well with the middle-term goal of using that to replace formal performance appraisals (or at least to reduce the effort for producing them).

Many of these practices enhance a culture of intense feedback loops. In many situations, however, it isn't entirely clear what professional feedback looks like. Table 6 reminds you what to keep in mind when you prepare to give feedback to a peer.

Giving Feedback	How?	Why?
Personal	I talk about my subjective impressions.	To emphasise that it is just one point of view.
Descriptive	Talk about concrete events, not about general ideas or judgments.	To make it easier to understand and accept.

Giving Feedback	How?	Why?
Timely	Close to a specific event.	To encourage learning.
Offering	Provide a different perspective, which is definitely not the right one.	To show respect even if you disagree.

Table 6: How to give professional feedback.

There are tons of guidelines available for how to professionally give and receive feedback. If there is no specific sense of urgency behind your feedback, try the "feedback and feed-forward" worksheet (see page 131), which has paid off for many groups.

For more confrontational dialogues, Paul Jerome's "feedback planner" (1999) on page 132 and the worksheet for tricky situations (see page 133) might be helpful. Both are clearly structured approaches that lead from a better understanding of yourself and of the specific context to questions and feedback that encourage explicit agreements for the future. You should keep a few prerequisites in mind when considering confronting a tricky situation:

- Take time for preparation. If you want to raise critical issues, you should especially be clear about your own emotional make-up.
- Be clear about what you want to achieve. If you want more than just talk, set your goal and clarify your strategy for the conversation.
- Have all the data you need to focus on the real problems. Again, don't rely on emotions or general impressions. Be as precise as possible.
- Focus on solutions. There is no sense in focusing too much on problems. Create multiple options if possible but do not push them on your colleague(s).
- Set the right tone by mindfully balancing asking, listening, and telling. Go first and model the behaviours you want to see for having a good conversation on bad things.
- Agree on the outcome of your conversation. Be clear about what the next step looks like.

It pays off to agree on a specific preparation tool before you start your conversation. If there is no agreement on the need for preparation, the focus on specific data, or the practice of active listening, chances are that your conversation will turn out to be a waste of time. All team members have to be clear both about how to provide and how to receive feedback. Table 7 provides a short reminder of the key pillars of the latter.

Receiving Feedback	How?	Why?
Active listening	Listen mindfully, paraphrase and summarise your understanding.	To discover the full message.
Clarifying	Ask questions for clarification.	To encourage learning.
Give yourself time to digest	Separate understanding from processing the feedback.	To prevent yourself from justifying or neglecting.
Appreciative	Thank the other one for her/his effort to help you.	To appreciate the attention and time.

Table 7: How to professionally receive feedback.

Whether feedback is exchanged on a one-on-one basis, within your team, or among different teams, make sure that your focus is on process and behaviour rather than on blame and guilt. Toyota's no-blame focus may help you to check your underlying assumptions (Rother 2009):

- People are doing their best.
- A problem is a system problem, and if we were the other person, the same problem would still have occurred.
- There is a reason for everything, and we can work together to understand the reason for a problem.

Changes on the organisational level

Many changes on the individual and the team levels involve other teams, functional departments, or even the whole organisation. In other words, they are systemic rather than local. This becomes crystal clear as soon as teams and managers focus on impediments beyond the given boundaries. This is one of the reasons why we have to bother with organisational change in a workbook about leading self-organising teams. On the one hand, organisational changes often alter the conditions under which self-organising teams interact, i.e. they change the whole container rather than just the interactions within this container. On the other hand, self-organising teams are an excellent means for effectively managing organisational change.

There is a simple rule of thumb for organisational change: the bigger the initiative, the higher the risk that it will fail. Change is always unpredictable but it's even harder to succeed on a broader level. What's the trouble with change? Why is it so hard to manage sustainable change throughout your enterprise? Summarising my own experience in multiple change initiatives, I see mainly three reasons for their high failure rate:

Change is not properly understood.

People affected by the change are not involved.

There is no effective system in place to establish a smooth change flow.

This deserves a bit of an explanation. Once again, in order to effectively overcome the failure patterns, we have to understand their root causes.

1. Change is not properly understood

That change is not properly understood often has a trivial reason: it is simply not visible. Especially in large organisations, nobody seems to know what is really going on in terms of change.

In addition to the transparency issue, the case for action is often unclear. Why do we need to change in the first place? Why now? Where does the case for action come from? How urgent is it? What is likely to happen if we do not change? In many cases, people neither understand the reason for change nor what is expected of them. In most cases, the lack of understanding is caused by an old-fashioned approach to change.

Still, many companies stick to the classic big-design up-front approach. The bigger the initiative, the more planning is involved, usually resulting in waterfall change projects with their well-known ingredients of fixed stages, predefined milestones, pushing things, hierarchical reporting structures, and the like. In other words, there is little room for agility.

The change is designed behind closed doors and is then pushed on to people.

No doubt, even if this approach has ever worked well, we need a new one for the 21st century. Increasing complexity, overwhelming dynamics, rampant uncertainty are just three of the many challenges current change initiatives have to cope with. There is far too much unknown territory to make any detailed up-front planning a valuable investment. But can we overcome our obsession with plans? How can we create a system capable of dealing with the intense change dynamics we are facing? What does a proper approach beyond planning look like?

If you don't see the forest for the trees

Working for the CTO of an international telecommunications company, I discovered seven different change initiatives running simultaneously: two initiatives for process improvement; two training and coaching projects for enhancing leadership competence; one workshop series for cultural integration following a merger; one team-building program for all implementation teams; and last but not least the introduction of kanban in one of these teams.

Much to the surprise of the CTO, the initial goals of two of the initiatives were changed while we worked to create a monitoring system. The priority of improving agile product management and a complementary agile leadership development program for management was swept away with the tide. Without our visual change-management system, nobody would have noticed how fast things were actually changing. If you cannot see what is going on, it is really hard to understand, let alone buy into, the change.

Usually, I address these questions with two strategies. The so-called "start with what you do now" method I introduced in the chapter on designing and the format of change teams. The first element follows the idea of evolutionary change management: it starts with respecting the current situation, understanding why we need further improvement, and determining what the next steps can look like. The second element explicitly builds on self-organising teams.

Figure 30: A change team starts with a retrospective of former initiatives.

A change team is defined as a group of key players who are responsible for the successful implementation of organisational change. Depending on the nature of the change you have in mind, this group can consist of both line managers and subject-matter experts in business processes, operations, and change management. I have had good experiences with this kind of a cross-functional, hierarchy-bridging, guiding coalition of members that:

- mindfully clarify their mission and boundaries;
- devote enough time to systematically unleash the power of a self-organising team, building the necessary trust and proactively addressing and resolving any blockers of change;
- understand themselves as role models for the change they want to see in place;
- create a proper system to manage change by applying good practices of self-organising teams such as visualising, limiting change in progress, making policies explicit, and establishing regular feedback loops;
- start with a retrospective of former change initiatives in order to distil lessons learned for the current initiative (see figure 30); and

- focus on the active involvement of all relevant stakeholders of the change process.
- The guidelines on how to set up a change team (page 134) should help you to make the most of it by creating the right container with the right mixture of people to encourage the necessary exchanges.

2. People affected by the change are not involved

The focus on stakeholder management leads us to the second failure pattern. Many initiatives still suffer from a lack of involvement. In other words, people affected by the change are neither accurately identified nor professionally involved. Since any corporate culture is strongly influenced by its external stakeholders, any culture-aware change effort should involve the relevant stakeholders as early as possible. Effectively involving stakeholders starts with identifying, grouping, and selecting those individuals and groups who are most affected by your specific initiative. I have good experience with visually mapping these stakeholders, which makes your assumptions as explicit as possible. The big picture you create enables fresh insights in the complex fields of power, communication, and relationships (see the guidelines for stakeholder mapping on page 135).

Your own perception is not enough though, because any self-awareness always encompasses some blind spots. In order to improve our cultural awareness, the next step is getting in touch with the most important stakeholders you have identified. Why should we involve our stakeholders? There is a simple yet convincing answer: "People do not resist change so much as they resist being changed. People are better at coping with change if they have a hand in creating it." (Manns and Rising 2004, p.11)

If you want to set the wheels of learning in motion, emotions are what you get. Changes can call for a broad spectrum of emotions: negative ones such as uncertainty, anger, and disappointment but also positive ones such as curiosity, joy, and enthusiasm. Even in a self-organising environment, team members can suffer quite intense periods of anxiety when it comes to organisation change. Many things can fuel these feelings:

- threat of loss of status ("Tomorrow, I won't be a manager anymore");
- devaluing your own expertise ("Tomorrow, all my experience as project manager will be worthless!);

- threat of dissolution of a well-known environment ("Tomorrow, I'll be working with a completely new team!");
- fear of feeling temporarily incompetent ("I simply can't do that");
- expectation of sanctions due to the incompetence ("If I don't manage it, I'll lose my position!"); or
- frustration at no longer belonging to a particular group or community ("What if I suddenly lose the connection to my colleagues?").

Fortunately, there are many ways to manage the risk of paralysing our teammates or other stakeholders with multiple anxieties. Creating the right container for change and involving those who are affected are good strategies. Sense of humour is another one that pays off in various situations.

Humour in change management

Since change processes are full of surprises, they are often met with laughter. This is not only due to the unexpected results that change often brings and the irritations it triggers, but also to funny observations and a good atmosphere. Our creed is that change management without humour is pointless. In relaxed situations, anyone can easily laugh. But humour is particularly helpful with the tougher aspects of change: we can discuss serious issues less threateningly, communicate important messages more easily, and break down deadly serious resistance with hearty laughter. Interestingly, the "ha ha" of laughter, the "aha" of comprehension, and the "ah" of discovery are essentially three aspects of the same exclamation.

As soon as you start to ask stakeholders for their points of view in order to better understand the current situation, you start to co-create your change initiative. In this regard, I recommend conducting a series of stakeholder interviews to explore the situation and the specific demands for a better future. I also recommend balancing these questions with focus on not only dissatisfactions and possible root causes but on positive aspects as well. What works well? What are you satisfied with? What can we build on? As the guidelines for stakeholder interviews document (see page 137), this balanced approach is driven by the necessary respect for the existing culture while preparing for evolutionary improvements.

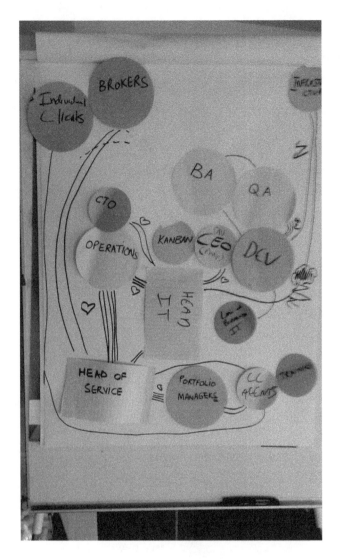

Figure 31: A sample stakeholder map.

A balanced approach to change

The figure in this box shows what this outcome can look like. It summarises the most important strengths and weaknesses, determined by the stakeholders of the IT-infrastructure department of a German energy supplier.

The change team that had conducted the interviews throughout the organisation built some clusters around the top three answers (red box) and highlighted some striking contradictions (box with lightning bolt). Consequently, they asked themselves how the envisioned implementation of Kanban would build on the strengths and address the weaknesses. In a short workshop, the team members presented both the interview outcomes and how they thought Kanban should help according to stakeholder input. By keeping their requirements transparent, they built trust and got explicit agreement on the Kanban implementation.

Strenghts	Weaknesses
> Flexibility	> Lack of coordination and structure
> Collaboration / Teamwork	> Prioritisation
> Know-How / Competency	> Predictability
> Engagement	> Back-Ups
> Innovation	> Conflict Daily Biz & Improvements
> Clear Processes	> Lack of documentation
> Quick Responses	> Many Delays
> Business Orientation	> Lack of Understanding (Change Requests)

There is a welcome side effect to actively involving our most important stakeholders: it builds trust by showing respect and interest – which is the prerequisite of any buy-in for change. For instance, if stakeholders are supposed to allow us more freedom for self-organisation, they have to trust that we use it in their interest.

We usually emphasise this trust-building strategy with another feedback loop based on the outcome of our interviews. We make transparent what we have learned, what it means for our change initiative, and how we will address the demands of our stakeholders. Again, we focus on challenges as well as strengths in order to show how we want to use the benefits of the existing culture while changing for the better.

The interview is not the only way to engage your stakeholders. *Fearless Change* authors Mary Lynn Manns and Linda Rising (2005) suggest various patterns for introducing new ideas:

- Ask for help on an on-going basis from peers, informal opinion leaders local sponsors, experienced mentors, external coaches, senior-level gurus who attract additional people, and experts from other areas. The involvement of sceptics or resistors especially might help to build the right momentum for your initiative.

- Provide opportunities for casual talk about new ideas, e.g. brown-bag meetings or any other meeting where you can "do food" to create a more relaxed atmosphere.

- Use informal corridor politics to inform important stakeholders, get the buy-in for formal decisions, and provide a personal touch, focusing on how it can be personally useful and valuable to decision makers.

- Bring in change practitioners from other areas or even other organisations to learn more about their experiences and increase the credibility of your own ideas.

- Run small experiments to test the waters, deliberately involving stakeholders.

- Say thank you in the most sincere way you can to everyone who helps you.

3. There is no effective system in place to establish a smooth change flow

Unfortunately, even the most effective stakeholder management does not guarantee the success of your change efforts. As mentioned, one of the main tasks of any change team is to create a proper system to overcome the third failure pattern of change initiatives: the chronic lack of change flow.

The following three examples, of many, illustrate that we are obviously more concerned about starting than finishing:

- A team enthusiastically agrees on the pair-programming approach only to find out that the team members don't devote enough time to it.

- A service department creates a lot of clever ideas for better involving their customers but never realises any of them.

- A whole business unit starts an organisational "go agile" initiative that fails to overcome the traditional project-management paradigm.

How do we stop starting and start finishing? What should any change team focus on? What can be done to encourage flow rather than blockages?

I have experience with borrowing not just popular slogans but some core practices of evolutionary change management. The first practice I recommend is to make change as visible as possible. Jointly visualising your current change activities as well as the change process can do wonders. It is an easy way to achieve a common understanding of both change system and change flow. Moreover, it allows you to observe your current activities and it helps you to clarify your specific tasks and responsibilities. Depending on the respective flight level – i.e. whether you are focused on the team, department, value stream, portfolio, or the whole organisation – a visual change-management system can look quite different (Leopold 2013). If you start one specific change initiative, it can look as simple as figure 32.

Figure 32 shows the change board of a German IT service department that is keen to manage their change initiative with kanban. Starting with delegates with various areas of expertise, the change team created a visual change-management system to mindfully run the broad initiative.

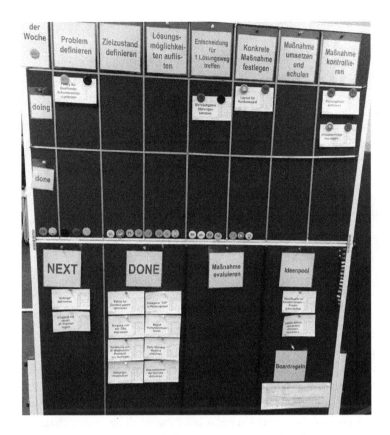

Figure 32: Change board of a German IT service department.

This system consists of process steps (in English, "Defining problems", "Clarifying goals", "Creating option", "Deciding on one option", "Defining measures", "Implementing measures", "Evaluating measures", and "Done"), change tickets (white sticky notes), avatars (coloured buttons with team members' initials), and a rotating "sponsor of the week" who is in charge of the change flow. Together with the department manager, this sponsor is also responsible for collecting new improvement ideas and decomposing them before they are selected for the next column. Part of the documented change policies (in the lower right corner) is to limit the number of measures to a maximum of five parallel tickets, each with two clearly identified ticket owners (shown by the coloured buttons on the tickets). This way, all team members are part of a change system that has already established a nice flow of small steps, as the tickets in the done column indicate.

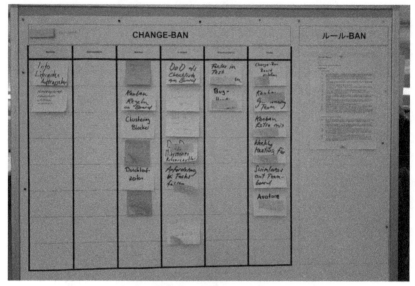

Figure 33: A change-ban board.

Figure 33 shows a different way to visualise the management of change. This so-called "change-ban board" of a Swiss IT-infrastructure department coordinates all improvement activities beyond the level of the four individual teams that all have kanban boards in place. Here, the leadership team, consisting of the department manager and his team leads, is responsible for the regular tracking of all on-going changes.

The board itself shows a process (the headings translate to "Backlog", "Selected", "Doing", "Communicating", and "Done"), tasks (yellow and blue sticky notes) and avatars (small orange sticky tabs). Although the board visualises what is currently going on ("start where you are") and even includes a collection of policies (the A4 sheet on the right), it also demonstrates a common problem: too much change in progress at once.

Figure 33 highlights the fact that demand regularly exceeds capability. This holds true for change management, too. Once we visualise what is going on, it becomes clear why traditional, push-driven change management is ineffective. There are far too many different initiatives in the change system. This explains why we are so busy with planning and starting rather than finishing initiatives – the well-known "good ideas instead of good results" syndrome. This explains why it is easy to get stuck or even lost in change. Simply speaking, change is far more about congestion management than flow. How can we overcome this syndrome? For sure, the evolutionary approach provides us a clear answer: limit change in progress (CIP), i.e. the number of parallel activities in order to foster effective flow.

Figure 34 shows both a radical way to implement a CIP limit and a creative way to visualise the change process. It is the so-called "improvement board" of an Austrian telecommunication company. The goal of this board is to track all on-going actions that help to improve collaboration between business and IT. Consequently, we have change agents from both sides that sponsor, run, and monitor various improvement activities.

The change process is defined by an input queue that is split between "collected" and "selected", and a PDCA-like cycle that runs through "prepare", "do", "feedback", and "adapt" until a specific change activity finally reaches the "done" column. Since business as well as IT had already suffered as a result of many unfinished initiatives, they decided to limit parallel activities to six items and the number of selected items to zero – which allowed them to shift their full attention to the loop-like flow and consistent completion of what they had already started.

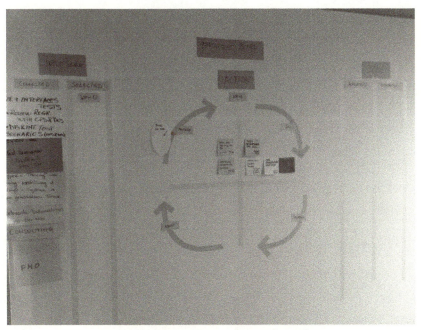

Figure 34: An improvement board.

In order to support a decent change flow, they also defined explicit policies and used blockers and avatars to make both activists and cases for action as clear as possible. One of the policies asked for starting as small as possible. Similar to starting small on the level of personal change, team and organisational changes can be focused on relatively simple experiments rather than complex initiatives. Robert Schaffer and Ron Ashkenas's concept for *Rapid Results!* (2005), Jeff Anderson's adoption of minimum viable changes (2012) or Jason Little's design for experiments (2014) all point in the same direction, having in common a cycle of: 1) starting with ideas, hypotheses, or insights; 2) creating and testing a new service or product increment; and 3) learning from professionally facilitated feedback loops in terms of conversations and metrics. To minimise the effort of planning, you can design each experiment by creating a simple canvas with the most important pillars. Canvases, such as the two shown on page 139, can be treated as living documents to be updated with every new cycle in which you learn more about what works and what doesn't. The visualisation encourages change flow in various ways by:

- focusing on actions and results than planning and preparation;
- strengthening self-organising capabilities such as designing and facilitating;
- building capacity and confidence experiments;
- testing large-scale change initiatives with low risks; and
- encouraging accountability and ownership at all levels of your organisation.

PART
FIVE

Tools for focusing

This section provides questionnaires, checklists, and guidelines for strengthening your focus. You can use these tried and tested tools in various ways:

- to learn new things or remind yourself of things you may have forgotten;
- to map these things with your current practice;
- to create fresh ideas for your daily business;
- to run some experiments; or
- to put the wheels of learning into motion.

As described in the chapter on the core capability of focusing, the tools should be applied with a systemic mind-set, i.e. with regard to the organisational context and the team situation at hand. The section starts the most important thing any self-organising team should focus on: the customer. To identify your customers and what they care about is often not trivial. A shared team mission statement is another way to clarify your purpose and how a customer benefits from the products and/or services you deliver. In addition, a shared vision statement at the level of department or business unit may provide the needed direction and guidance for strategic decision making.

The questionnaire in "Catch you if you can" shifts the focus to the necessary self-awareness. The guidelines in "Sharing perspectives on the team", "Levels of team communication", "Decision-making policies", and "Managing the unexpected" should help you and your team to develop an agile mind-set and build reliable organisations. Finally, "Deciphering your company culture" describes an exercise to help you to better understand your corporate culture and how it shapes the way you do things on your team.

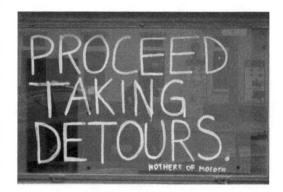

Identify your customers and what they care about

Take some time to check the following questions. Inspired by Steven Spear, these questions may help you if you are:

about to form a new team;

doubt whether you are still focusing on the right things;

in trouble with your customer relationships; or

curious to learn more about your team's main purpose.

Make this an effective team building activity. Let all team members write their answers on sticky notes and cluster the answers to identify commonalities and similarities.

Who are our customers?

What do our customers need?

What are their specific expectations?

What do we need to fulfil or even exceed these expectations?

How do we effectively create value for them?

How do we stream the process of value creation?

Team mission statement

///

A clear mission statement for your team defines:

- what your purpose is;
- who is on your team;
- what you deliver; and
- how a customer benefits.

Your mission statement provides a short summary of the what, why, how, and who of the products and services your team has to offer.

You can create the necessary building blocks for your own mission by answering the following questions:

- What is the fundamental purpose, the reason for existence of your team? If in doubt, use the "five why" approach in which you start with a descriptive statement about your team and then ask "Why is it important?" After asking why a maximum of five times, you are likely to arrive at the fundamental purpose.
- Who are your customers?
- Who is on your team?
- What do you deliver to your customers?
- How do these deliverables contribute to your customeŕs success?

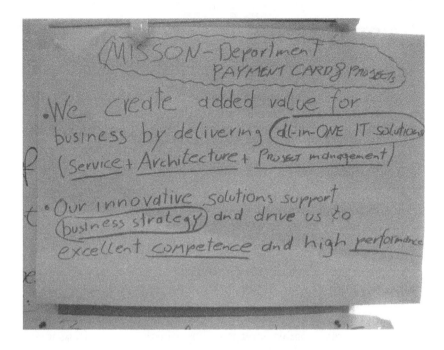

Figure 35: The mission statement of an IT marketing team.

Vision statement

A vision is an idealised picture of the future of your business and your organisation. As such it is a combination of three basic elements:

- an organisation/department/team mission statement;
- its core purpose and core values; and
- the "big picture" aspirations for the future.

Usually, a powerful vision statement is the first step in strategic planning. A vision shared by all the members of your organisational unit helps to set goals and clarify your internal organisation.

In order to create the necessary building blocks for your powerful vision, the following structure has proven to be helpful.

It is 5/10/15/X years from today and you have, marvellously enough, created your most desirable enterprise. Describe that enterprise as if you are able to see it around you:

- How has the business environment changed?
- Who is part of your business in 5/10/15/X years? Who are your employees, stakeholders, and partners?
- Who are your current customers? What can you do for them that will contribute to their success?
- What new challenges do you have to handle?
- How does your enterprise differ from that of your competitors? What makes you unique?

Catch you if you can

//

This questionnaire helps you to explore how you climb up the ladder of inference. Start from below and go up rung by rung.

Ladder rungs	Questions	Answers (keywords)
Actions	What actions did I take?	
Beliefs	What general beliefs did I adopt or confirm?	
Conclusions	What specific conclusions did I draw?	
Assumptions	What did I assume?	
Meaning	What did the selected data mean to me?	
Selection	Where did I focus?	
"Reality"	What was the situation I am focusing on like?	

Having reconstructed how you climbed up the ladder of inference, try to catch yourself by looking for obvious gaps and contradictions. Point out questionable selections, false assumptions, and over-generalisations. Finally, focus on questions such as:

- How did the way I climbed up the ladder of inference impact the situation?
- What did it mean to others and me such as peers, team(s), and management?
- How familiar does this ladder climb feel?
- What would an improvement step look like?

Sharing perspectives on the team

Diversity experts Lee Gardenswartz and Anita Rowe (2003) provide a list of ideas for warming up by exploring commonalities and differences. Here is how it works.

Pair up with someone on your team (preferably someone you don't know well) and take turns responding to one or more of the open-ended statements below.

You can provide your favourite statements to the team or let them decide what resonates most with them, e.g. by doing a quick dot-vote.

In addition, you can decide whether or not you want everyone to write a summary, you want to facilitate a callout, or you want to stop at the one-on-one conversations.

The statements:

- What I like best about being on this team is...
- I'm most frustrated in the group when...
- I feel most part of the team when...
- I try to include others by...
- I feel left out on the team when...
- A strength I bring to the team is...
- A major problem or obstacle on our team is...
- I work best with people who...
- I'd be a better team member if...
- Our team works best when...
- Our team gets blocked when...
- One thing I wish others on the team knew or understood about me is...
- I'd be happier on this team if...
- An accomplishment of the team I'm most proud of is...
- Getting ahead on this team means...
- I get nervous on the team when...
- I'm most stimulated and energised on the team when...
- One of the smartest moves we made was...
- One of the biggest mistakes we made was...
- Something I'd love to see our team accomplish is...

Levels of team communication

In order to keep the momentum of consistent team building, professional communication is key. The following overview will kindly remind you that different levels of communication have to be balanced in order to focus on the right things.

OPERATIONAL COMMUNICATION	
Focus on daily business	**Key questions**
Goals	What are we busy with at the moment?
Results	
	What works? What doesn't?
Work processes	
	What impedes or blocks us?
Problems and constraints	
	How do we handle these things?
Information flow	
	Who is doing what?
Decision making	

STRATEGIC COMMUNICATION	
Focus on business development	**Key questions**
Demand	What have we achieved so far?
Value-creation processes	How does the customer benefit from what we deliver?
Future plans	
	What does the feedback from the customer look like?
Connection between teams	
Silo and hierarchy-bridging communication	What can we build on?
Decision making	Where do we see the biggest areas for improvement?

SELF-REFLECTIVE COMMUNICATION

Focus on teamwork and leadership	Key questions
Culture of collaboration	What are we happy with? What are we proud of?
Climate on and around the team	
Observations and feelings	What frustrates us? What feels embarrassing?
Commonalities and differences	What do we appreciate of one another?
Tensions and conflicts	
Decision making	What would we like to see changed?

Decision-making policies

//

How decisions are made and communicated is crucial for self-organising teams, which is why you find decision making at any level of communication. In line with systems theorist Niklas Luhmann (1995), we could even go assert that the basic driver of self-organisation is the effective communication of decisions.

Encouraging leadership at all levels doesn't necessarily mean that the team decides everything on its own. On the contrary, being clear about the different modes of decision making is part of any professional boundary setting. In most cases, it seems to be enough for managers to distinguish four modes of decision making:

1. Hierarchical decisions

"The problem is the following.... Here is what the solution should look like.... I want you to implement this solution."

This policy should be in place for all decisions regarding the container and its context (see the C/D/E model in the chapter "What are self-organising teams?").

2. Consultative decisions

"The problem is the following.... I need your help to create the right solution. What do you think we should do?"

This policy pays off for all decisions for which the manager needs input from the team. A classic example is finding the best options for dealing with stakeholder interests. The manager, however, takes full responsibility for making the final decision.

3. Joint decisions

"The problem is the following.... I want us to find what the best solution looks like and make a decision together."

This policy declares shared responsibility of both the manager and the team. This policy makes sense for all decisions regarding product strategy or cross-boundary collaboration. In order to prevent confusion, the manager should be clear about how the final decision will be made by consensus, compromise, majority vote, or some other policy.

4. Team decisions

"The problem is the following.…. I want you to find the best solution and implement it."

Managers should be aware that this policy means that they have to live with whatever the team decides. In my understanding, this mode is needed for both technical and operational issues. Overruling or micro-managing is not an option and destroys the power of self-organisation.

Self-development

This assessment provides an opportunity to better understand what your current commitment to self-development looks like. Rate every statement, with 1 representing "I'm 100% focused on this" and 5 meaning no attention at all.

This assessment has been designed to encourage small experiments in areas where you feel you could improve the current situation. Ask yourself: "What can I do in this regard to achieve a 2 rather than a 3?"

In addition, you can use the same questionnaire to ask others for feedback. Let them – preferably people close to you – mark down their answers and compare them with your own.

My focus	1	2	3	4	5
I have already devoted much time to develop myself.					
I clearly understand what it means to start with myself.					
I strive for perfection although I know that humans are never perfect.					
I treat errors, mistakes, or unexpected events as opportunities to learn.					
I apply a self-critical attitude.					
When problems occur, I am willing to reflect on how I've possibly contributed to these problems.					
I feel and show a deep respect for more senior people who have invested a lot in developing themselves.					
I regularly ask for their point of view.					
I regularly ask for feedback from the people I work with.					
I explicitly ask for advice on where to improve.					
I take their advice as an opportunity to start small changing experiments.					
I mindfully evaluate my experiments by asking people around me for their perspectives.					

Managing the unexpected

In their landmark book on this topic, organisational psychologists Karl Weick and Kathleen Sutcliffe (2001) provide clear guidelines. Their intriguing case studies of so-called high-reliability organisations such as fire departments, nuclear power plants, and emergency rooms suggest a simple rule of thumb: the better we manage the unexpected, the better our capability to respond in an agile manner. Here is what we should keep in mind when developing teamwork capabilities.

ACTING WITH ANTICIPATION

Preoccupation with failure by:

- paying attention to failures, even to small errors and almost-accidents;
- generating lessons learned as fast as possible;
- analysing your behaviour honestly; and
- making good use of short-lived moments of learning.

Reluctance to simplify interpretations by:

- checking your basic assumptions on a regular basis;
- looking for disconfirming information;
- treating credibility and trust as perishable properties; and
- continually nurturing and renewing them if they are to survive.

Sensitivity to operations by:

- moving authority toward expertise, wherever it lies;
- relativizing hierarchy and seniority;
- migrating the designation of who is the relevant decision maker; and
- creating a climate where people feel safe to question assumptions and report problems.

CONTAINING THE UNEXPECTED WHEN IT OCCURS

Commitment to resilience by:

- preparing your team to manage the unexpected when it does happen;
- dealing actively with surprises;
- bouncing back from errors and coping with surprise in the moment; and
- using expert networks, an extensive action repertoire, and skills with improvisation.

Deference to expertise by:

- focusing on surprise and the unexpected;
- using as much information as possible;
- minding distortion and tunnel vision; and
- pushing decision-making authority down – and around.

Deciphering your company culture

In *The Corporate Culture Survival Guide,* Ed Schein provides a four-hour exercise for assessing your culture (2009, p.83). Here are the building blocks of this exercise.

1. **Meet in a comfortable room** with enough wall space, materials for visualisation, and a setup that encourages face-to-face conversation (e.g. a chair circle).

2. **State the business problem** (this should take 30 minutes). Why do you need to assess your culture?

3. **Review the concept of culture and its levels** (15 minutes). Help everybody to understand that the assessment is about identifying what supports the proposed solution of your business problem and detecting possible impediments due to unmanaged contradictions between artefacts, espoused values, and shared tacit assumptions.

4. **Identify artefacts** (60 minutes). What is characteristic for your organisation? List typical things such as architecture, dress codes, working hours, meetings, decision-making policies, learning concepts, rituals, work/life balance, and the like. In short, basically list everything you can see, hear, or somehow feel.

5. **Identify your organisation's espoused values** (30 minutes): Make another list for the values that your organisation holds. What does your enterprise officially care about? The values may be part of your official vision or any official statement about "What is most important to us."

6. **Compare values with artefacts** (60 minutes): Crosscheck your list of artefacts against the values. For example, if customer focus is espoused as a value, see what systems of reward or accountability you have identified as artefacts and whether those support customer focus. If they do not, you have identified an area in which a contradiction assumption is in place. Identify what is really driving the behaviours in your company. Write this assumption on another sheet.

7. **Assess the shared assumptions** (45 minutes). Find things that will aid or hinder you in activating a solution for the problem you set out in the first step of your meeting. Focus most of your energy on identifying the assumption that can help you. If you detect real constraints, you must make a plan to change those elements of the culture.

8. **Decide next steps** (45 minutes). Draw conclusions and agree on next steps. What can you build on? What needs to change? What can a next step in culture evolution look like?

If the result of your exercise feels incomplete or muddy, repeat the process with one or more other groups. Gather a diverse mix of people to make the most out of it. Exploring different points of view of the whole elephant always pays off.

PART SIX

Tools for designing

In this section, I provide questionnaires, checklists, and guidelines for strengthening your designing capability. You can use these tried and tested tools in various ways:

- to learn new things or remind yourself of things you may have forgotten;
- to map these things to your current practice;
- to develop fresh ideas for your daily business;
- to run experiments; and
- to put the wheels of learning into motion.

As described in the chapter on the core capability of designing, the tools should be applied with a systemic mind-set, i.e. in regard to the organisational context and the team situation at hand. The section starts and ends with a simple questionnaire. "Micro-management assessment" and "Macro-management assessment" are like brackets that encompass various opportunities for systemic design of both workflow and management role. Within these brackets, you find guidelines and checklists for clarifying your current whereabouts and the prerequisites for moving on. "Start with what you do now", "Clarify where you start", and "Prerequisites for the design of your Kanban system" all focus on a pragmatic, nevertheless differentiated assessment of your current situation that is often neglected. "Design your team charter", "Design your visual work-management system", "Design your role as a manager", and "Design your action review cycle" offer step-by-step guidelines for coming up with better solutions to your current problems. They encourage you to focus on your strengths and capabilities in order to use them wisely for continuous improvement.

Micro-management assessment

The following assessment provides an opportunity to better understand where you start from as a manager. It is a simple list of statements to help you to identify individual strengths and weaknesses. Rate every statement from 1 representing "I'm 100% focused on this" to 5 meaning no attention at all.

This assessment has been designed to encourage small experiments in areas where you feel like you should make a difference to the current situation. Ask yourself, "What can I do in this regard to achieve a 2 rather than a 3?"

My focus	1	2	3	4	5
Daily business is at the centre of my attention.					
I am busy fulfilling all my tasks.					
I help my team(s) wherever I can.					
I am the single point of contact for our most important stakeholders.					
I do everything I can to protect my team from external interventions.					
As soon as I realise what is needed at the moment, I do it.					
I have established a system for regular status reports.					
I facilitate all meetings.					
Team members are obliged to escalate problems as soon as possible.					
I have regular one-on-one conversations with all team members.					
I have a clear set of metrics to measure everyone's performance.					
I conduct regular performance appraisals with each team member.					
I have defined KPIs for assessing each team member.					

Compare your results with those from the questionnaire in "Macro-management assessment" at the end of this tools section. In addition, you can use the same questionnaire to ask others for feedback. Let them – preferably people close to you – write their answers and compare them to your own.

Start with what you do now

Here are some questions, inspired by Mike Burrows (2014), to help you better understand your current situation.

What is the purpose of your system?

How does it serve the customer?

How does it work for those inside the system?

What can you build on? What positive feedback do you receive from customers?

What leaves your customers or other stakeholders dissatisfied and yourself frustrated?

How can these things be changed safely?

Service orientation can also be improved on a smaller scale. Let the team answer for each problem:

1. What solutions to the problem has the team considered?

2. What, specifically, have your peers (and others impacted) agreed to do?

3. In what ways does the customer benefit?

4. How does this look from the organisation's perspective?

5. Are we solving the right problem?

Design your team charter

The team charter is a summary of the key pillars of a self-organising team. It helps you to define all the building blocks necessary to run a successful as well as satisfying business.

Here are some guidelines for creating a joint team charter:

- Explain the purpose and potential benefits of a team charter.
- Achieve agreement if you want to create a charter and carry it out.
- Take some time off the job and provide professional facilitation.
- Give everybody the chance to contribute and distil the most important answers to the basic questions.

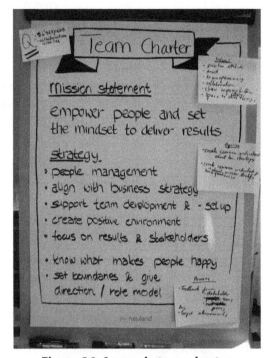

Figure 36: A sample team charter.

- Seek final commitment to holding each other accountable for following the charter.
- Display the charter, best as a physical artefact, in a visible location.
- Check the charter on a regular basis (e.g. within retrospectives) and treat it as a living document that can be changed continuously.

How to measure anything

In his intriguing book on measuring, Douglas Hubbard (2014) recommends **putting measurement in context** whenever confronted with apparently complex topics that cause uncertainty. Prior to making a measurement, we need to answer the following:

- What is the focus of our measurement?
- What decision is it supposed to support?
- What is the definition of the thing being measured in terms of observable consequences?
- How exactly does this thing matter to the decision being asked? How do we compute outcomes based on the value of this variable?
- How much do we know about it now? What is our current level of uncertainty)?
- How does uncertainty about this variable create risk for the decision? Is there a threshold value, above which one action is preferred and below which another is preferred?
- What is the value of additional information?

In addition, Hubbard encourages us to look for existing research on the topic. In most cases, we don't have to start from scratch. Most of what self-organising teams and managers care about, like productivity, performance, quality, risk, or customer satisfaction, has been measured before. Before you reinvent the wheel, do your homework; see what the Internet has to provide. In larger organisations, it may pay off to ask other teams or peers for help, too.

We can make good use of simple rules such as the **rule of five**: there is a 93.75% chance that the median of a population falls between the smallest and the largest values of any five random samples of a population. The **single-sample majority rule** states that if you believe the proportion of values in your population could be anything from 0% to 100% with all values being equally likely, that there is a 75% chance that any single random sample is from the majority of the population.

As Hubbard points out, you almost always have far more data than you think while actually needing far less data than you think. Useful, new observations are more accessible than you think. Unfortunately, many managers tend to start each problem from scratch. Fortunately this is easy to fix. "Again, when you know next to nothing, you don't need much additional data to tell you something you didn't know before." (*ibid* 2014, p.64)

Clarify where you start

The following questionnaire has already been used with many clients. Klaus Leopold and I (2015) designed it to help you clarify the current situation at the beginning of a possible kanban implementation.

We highly recommend you answer all questions before you proceed.

1. We have identified the area where we want to implement kanban.

   The following parts of the value chain should be improved:

2. We agree that there is a sense of urgency for change.

   Our three most important challenges are:

   1.

   2.

   3.

3. We are convinced that kanban will help us solve our current problems.

   Particularly, the following kanban elements address these problems:

   The following questions are still open for us:

4. We have identified the key stakeholders who are responsible for the success of our change initiative.

    The key stakeholders are:

5. We have a clear understanding of how our key stakeholders will respond to the kanban initiative and what we need to do to get their commitment.

    We will get the commitment of our stakeholders by:

6. We know who will lead the change initiative (who will be the change agents) and provide appropriate resources for them.

    These agents and resources are:

7. We have learned our lessons in change management and know what we are going to do better than in previous initiatives.

    Here are our most important ideas for improvement:

8. We expect specific constraints in our improvement initiative and have a plan how to deal with them.

    The three most important constraints we expect are:

    1.

    2.

    3.

    How we want to deal with these constraints:

Prerequisites for the design of a kanban system

As experience shows, it pays off to check whether you have everything you need before kicking off your design process. This checklist should help you:

Prerequisites	Yes	No
We have identified where we want to design a kanban system.		
We have a common understanding why we want to do that.		
We have properly involved those who are affected by our initiative.		
Those who are supposed to run the system have been trained in the principles and practices of visual work management.		
We asked all relevant stakeholders for their feedback on the strengths and weaknesses of our current work-management system.		
They understand how they benefit from the new system.		
They know what will be different for them in the future.		
They explicitly agreed to try it.		
We have a prioritised list with the most important things we can further build on and what we should improve.		
We have decided who will be designing the system.		
We have got all materials needed for our design (a board, sticky notes, cards, markers, tape, index strips, magnets, and the like).		
We have decided where we want to place our board.		
We have a plan how we want to involve those who are affected, get feedback on our draft design, improve, and kick it off.		

I highly recommend thinking twice before you ignore a "No". It might not block you right now – for instance, not to properly involve your stakeholders – but could have a serious impact on operation.

Design your visual work-management system

Here is a step-by-step guide that Klaus Leopold and I designed (2015) to lead you from reviewing the current demand to the specific design of your visual work-management system.

1. Identify work types:

Who is demanding which kind of work?

What is most valuable for our customer?

To whom do we deliver our work once we are done?

2. Identify the workflow:

- What are typical steps in our process?
- How do we create value with each work item?

3. Define WIP limits:

- How much work can be done in parallel?
- What is needed to encourage workflow?

4. Define classes of service:

- What is the business impact of the respective work types?
- What is the risk behind the individual work items?

5. Define metrics:

- What do we have to measure in order to learn more about our true capabilities?

6. Define meetings:

- What coordination is needed?
- How can we set a cadence of meetings to save cost?

Design your role as a manager

Here is another step-by-step guide to increase the fitness of your role in a lean and agile environment.

1. Review your current situation as a manager:
- What works well? What are you happy with?
- What does not work well? What puzzles or embarrasses you?
- What are the root causes of your current situation?

2. Clarify how you add value as a manager:
- How do you contribute to satisfying the customer?
- How do you contribute to your team's achievements?
- How do you contribute to your company´s overall success?

3. Ientify what is actually needed:
- What services do you deliver?
- What kind of expectations do you fulfil?
- What is needed from your side?

4. Define classes of service:
- What is the business impact of your services?
- Who benefits from what you are doing?
- What is the risk behind the specific services you are delivering?

5. Map with existing roles:
- Who should be accountable for what kind of services?
- How many roles are needed?

6. Define how to align the different leadership roles:
- What coordination is needed?
- How do you encourage leadership at all levels?

7. Define feedback loops:
- How do you measure whether you are doing a good job?

Design your action review cycle

The action review cycle (ACR) places so-called bookends before and after each important unit of action (see Parry, Pires, and Guber 2007). In the tradition of lean and agile meetings, both the before action review (BAR) and after action review (AAR) should be short and structured.

The focus of BARs is on explicitly articulating and aligning your plans before going into action. In the AARs, initial hypotheses are tested against data from the executed action. Once established and professionally facilitated, this feedback cycle makes learning almost inevitable and accountability visible.

Before action review	After action review
Focus: Alignment and readiness for effective action	Focus: Accountability and actionable insights
What are our intended results and metrics?	What was our intent and plan?
What challenges can we anticipate?	What were the actual results?
What did we/others learn in similar situations?	What caused these results and any gaps?
What will make the biggest difference?	What will I/we sustain and improve?

Macro-management assessment

The following assessment provides an opportunity to better understand where you start from as a manager. It is **a simple list of statements to help you identify individual strengths and weaknesses.** Rate every statement from 1 representing "I'm 100% focused on this" to 5 meaning no attention at all. This assessment has been designed to encourage small experiments in the areas where you feel like you could make a positive difference to the current situation. Ask yourself "What can I do to achieve a 2 rather than a 3?" Compare your results with the **micro-management assessment** provided at the beginning of this tools section. You can also use this questionnaire to ask others for feedback. Let them preferably people close to you – mark their answers, and then you should compare them to your own.

My focus	1	2	3	4	5
Value adding is at the centre of my attention.					
I have defined a clear catalogue of leadership services.					
I focus not just on my team(s) but also on the end-to-end value stream.					
I continuously align with my peers in the value stream.					
I do whatever I can to provide clear boundaries for my team(s).					
I empower my team(s) by giving freedom to act.					
I provide enough opportunities to increase our capabilities.					
I understand the concept of leadership as a team sport and do whatever I can to encourage leadership at all levels.					
I provide a supportive context in terms of information, education, and reward.					
I set clear decision-making authorities.					

My focus	1	2	3	4	5
We set a cadence of meetings to coordinate our efforts.					
We agreed on some metrics to measure our progress.					
I am aware of potential contradictions between what I practice and what I preach.					
I regularly ask for feedback on my role.					
I am 100% committed to self-development and continuous improvement.					

PART
SEVEN

Tools for facilitating

This section provides questionnaires, checklists, and guidelines for strengthening your facilitating ability. You can use these proven tools in various ways:

- to learn new things or remind yourself of things you may have forgotten;
- to map these things with your current practice;
- to create fresh ideas for your daily business;
- to run experiments; and
- to put the wheels of learning into motion.

As argued in the chapter on facilitating, the tools should be applied with a systemic mind-set, i.e. in regard to the organisational context and the team situation at hand. The section starts with a sample interview guideline for the appreciative-inquiry approach. Thus, it starts with one idea for facilitating one-on-one conversations in order to build trust. Humble inquiry has the same goal and offers a bridge between one-on-one and team conversations. The guidelines for facilitating go-arounds and for chart writing may serve as a kind reminder that respect and appreciation are also a matter of professionalism.

The main part of the section is on facilitating various feedback loops: regular stand-up, product review, operations review, and the retrospective are well-known formats in the lean agile environment. However, I decided to include these tools here because they are essential drivers of a culture of continuous improvement that is hopefully not limited to lean, XP, Scrum, Kanban or any other method, and because, reflecting on my own messy routines, I thought the tools might be helpful for practitioners either getting started or looking for fresh ideas for further improvement.

Finally, I added some guidelines for large-group events and three of my favourite formats: world café, open space, and lean coffee. Although designed as catalysts for self-organisation on a broader level, these formats also work well in most team environments.

Appreciative inquiry

As introduced in the chapter on facilitating, the partner interview is at the heart of the appreciative-inquiry approach. Let people pair up, best with someone they don't know that well, and provide worksheets with questions to guide the interview. Have each member of a pair listen and take notes in turn (each interview should not take longer than 10-15 minutes). At the end, invite them to present their most important insights on sticky notes.

Here is one example of what the worksheet can look like:

Tell me about a key experience with leading teams.

Without being too humble, what do you most value about yourself and the way you lead teams? What are your personal strengths?

What do you see as key challenges for you as a team leader? What would you like to improve?

Humble inquiry

According to former MIT professor and organisational-culture expert Ed Schein (2013), humble inquiry is the gentle art of asking instead of telling. It is about asking questions to which you do not know the answer and building a relationship based on true interest in the other person. Here is a sample of questions you can use.

To start the conversation:
- What's happening?
- What's going on?
- So? (with an expectant look)
- Can you give me an example?

To get more diagnostic to learn more about feelings and reactions:
- How did you feel about that?
- How does that resonate with you?
- Did that arouse any reactions in you?

To clarify causes and motives:
- Why did that happen?
- Why did you feel that way?
- What may have caused this?
- Why do you suppose that happened?

To highlight actions:
- What have you tried so far?
- How did you get there?
- What did you do about that? (e.g. in response to a complaint)
- What are you going to do next?

To better understand systems:
- What did they do then?
- How do you think they felt when you did that?
- How would they have reacted if you had told them?
- What do you think they will do if you follow through on what you said?

To think outside the box:

- Imagine a miracle happens overnight and your problem is gone when you wake up. What would be different for you then? What would be different for your team, management, and customer?

- Imagine a fairy grants you three wishes in order to solve all your problems and create a perfect working situation. What exactly would you wish for?

Go-around

What is the go-around about?

The go-around is a simple yet effective means to activate the whole group by asking one question and inviting the team members to take turns answering this question.

Why do we need to go around?

Giving everybody the opportunity to speak serves multiple purposes:

- It helps to learn what is on everybody's mind.
- It focuses the group on listening.
- It ensures equal participation.
- It clarifies what the group is busy with the most.
- It sheds new light on the current situation.
- It is an easy means to gather diverse data before jumping to conclusions and actions.
- It is a catalyst for making better decisions.

How to make the most out of it?

Here are some rules you should be clear about before starting a go-around:

- There is only one question to be answered. To keep that in mind, I recommend you visualise this question on a sticky note or flip chart to focus everybody's attention.
- Everyone takes a turn to speak on the question without interruption or comment from others.
- To make this a quick round of expressing one's own opinion rather than a long list of arguments, you can set a specific time-box, e.g. a maximum of two minutes per person. Alternatively, you can limit the go-around to just one sentence or even a word, e.g. for an energising check-in or check-out.
- In addition, it is a good practice to set a speaking order either by starting with someone next to you or simply by asking who wants to start. Once the go-around begins, enforce a direction (clockwise or counter-clockwise) in which to "go around" to encourage a good flow of statements.

- Give the group some time to think before you start the go-around.
- Don't put too much pressure on people who are not able or willing to speak up. Allow them to pass their turn but come back to them after everybody else has spoken.
- Take a break if too many people pass. Give yourself time to think about possible reasons. Was it the wrong question? Wrong situation? Lack of trust?
- If in doubt, ask informally for help.

Chart writing

///

Professional facilitation needs professional documentation. Here are some tips to consider.

Write legibly:
- Use the wide end of the marker tip.
- Write big enough so that everyone in the room can read it. Write larger if the group is larger.
- Even when you are in a hurry, do your best to make thick-lined, closed letters and write in straight lines.

Sentences are easier to read:
- "Send a thank-you note to Bill" is much easier to understand than "note to Bill".
- Verbs and nouns take high priority; adjectives and adverbs are low priority.

Use the right colours:
- Use black and blue colours to record what has been said.
- Use red and green to highlight and structure.
- Use coloured cards to create background structure.

Use symbols:
- Use bullets, stars, borders, or arrows strengthen the impact of your record.

Prepare specific formats:
- Use a list, matrix, flowchart, diagram, or other prepared structure according to your expected outcomes.

Encourage proofreading:
- Invite people to read over your work. Accept corrections gladly. Even if these corrections mess up your beautiful chart, remember that this is how it becomes *their* chart.

Standup meeting

What is the stand-up meeting about?

The stand-up is a short meeting of all people responsible for a specific work system. The number of attendees and the cadence of the meeting depend on the complexity of this system.

Why this meeting?
- Coordinate daily business.
- Focus on workflow.
- Identify obstacles so people can take steps to remove them.
- Share commitment.
- Communicate directly.
- Encourage responsibility and leadership at all levels.

How to make the most out of it?
- All hands: try to replace as many additional meetings and reports as possible.
- Stand-up: link physical with mental readiness.
- Same place, same time: reduce coordination cost.
- Time-boxed: no longer than 15 minutes.
- Attend by proxy or delegate: if you are not available, have another team member report your status. If too many people would show up – usually, more than 20 – instead have each team send a delegate to attend the stand-up. But don't forget to have a policy for info flow and feedback in place.
- Focus on customer value, workflow, and blockers or impediments. A visual work management system makes it easier to keep focus and concentrate on the most important question: What does everybody have to know in order to make the right decisions?
- Take offline: only brief clarifying questions are allowed. Longer storytelling or problem solving has to take place outside the stand-up.
- Install clear communication policies to ensure self-organisation with respect to:
- Ownership: The stand-up is owned by all attendees, i.e. everyone working within a specific work system.

- Value: Check the return on time invested (ROTI) regularly. If attendees do not benefit from the meeting, you have an issue for further improvement.

- Attention: One speaker talks at a time. There are no side conversations. Each speaker talks to the whole group of attendees, not only to a senior boss, line manager, ScrumMaster, or kanban hero. Define a speaking order if necessary by passing a token, going clockwise, and the like.

Product review

//

What is the product review about?

The product review is a live demonstration of the latest product increment and invites customers and other stakeholders to critically review and provide feedback on what has been built so far.

Why do we need the product review?

The purpose of the meeting is to show what the team has accomplished and learn from feedback. The product review is one of the building blocks for establishing a system of fast feedback loops with your customer and so should be a regular meeting in any product development area s and not just in the Scrum world where it is an essential part of each sprint.

How to design and facilitate the product review?

In Scrum, the product owner often facilitates the meeting. In other contexts, often the product or a line manager feels the need to be in charge of the meeting. I strongly recommend that the team members themselves run the meeting since they are responsible for both the technical quality of the increment and its proper delivery.

In order to get the most out of a product review, the customers and stakeholders should review:

- the work completed according to the team's initial commitment – what works well, what does not, and why?;
- key decisions that were made during the latest iteration, whether they are technical or market-driven;
- essential performance metrics (speed, data quality, robustness, etc.);
- new customer requirements that have popped up during the last iteration; and
- priorities (for the next iteration.

This feedback loop is important for living up to the standards of agile development. Critical feedback and change requests of any sort are welcome and usually are not difficult to tackle. For teams, nevertheless, it is also important that the customer expresses positive feedback and accepts the work that fulfils his or her expectations. Sometimes, customers need more time to digest what they review before they formally accept the potential shipment.

The duration of the customer review meeting varies depending on the length of the latest iteration, the complexity of the increment, and the quality of the relationship, i.e. the trust that has been built so far. One to two hours, however, seems to be common sense.

Operations review

What is the operations review about?

The operations review is a meeting to focus on the overall performance of your system. This may be only your team or all teams of an entire value stream. Usually, all important stakeholders of this value stream gather to check performance data (e.g. throughput, lead times, failure rate, cost, revenue, etc.), ask questions, and provide feedback. Organisational issues such as systemic impediments and new business opportunities can also be addressed.

Why this meeting?

The operations review serves multiple purposes:

- making the team's performance transparent by focusing on objective data;
- providing a feedback loop for current achievements;
- clarifying what worked well and what should be done differently;
- driving continuous improvement at the enterprise or business-unit level;
- building trust among teams, managers, and their multiple stakeholders; and
- facilitating a vital component in developing organisational maturity.

How to design and facilitate the operations review?

To realise the full potential of this format, you should ensure that the meeting:

- is held regularly (usually in a monthly to quarterly cadence);
- takes only 60-90 minutes;
- is based on a well-structured agenda;
- builds on evidence-based input from multiple points of view including some guests from other areas;
- mindfully summarises all improvement measures that have been agreed on; and
- provides food and snacks to encourage attendance.

Retrospective facilitator's questionnaire

///

The following questionnaire should help you to prepare for your next retrospective or any other meeting format devoted to learn from the past in order to create a better future. Take your time to think about the questions and take some notes to make your ideas as explicit as possible.

QUESTIONS	NOTES
What do you want to achieve?	
What's required to achieve your goals?	
Who should participate?	
What do the conditions (venue, space, equipment, time) look like?	
Who is responsible for invitation, preparation, facilitation, documentation, and information follow-up?	
What policies do you have in place?	
How do you design your retrospective?	
How do you kick off?	
How do you encourage the right mind-set?	
How do you gather data?	
How do you generate insights?	
How do you decide what to do?	
What does your time management look like?	
How do you conclude and evaluate the retrospective?	
What needs to be documented?	
How do you follow up?	
Who will be informed about the results?	
How do you support implementation of your improvement experiments?	
How do you monitor your improvement process?	

Large group events

///

This expanded questionnaire should help you to keep overview when you are about to manage the complexity of a large-group event. I strongly recommend you take time to find answers before you start to manage.

Set the goals:

- What do you want to achieve? Why do you need a large-group event to achieve these goals?

Select the participants:

- Who should be part of the event?
- Who is needed to achieve the goals of the event?
- How do you deal with people who cannot attend?

Set the boundaries:

- When? How long? Where?
- Who is the sponsor or host of the event?
- Who is in charge of preparing, facilitating, and debriefing the event?
- How do you build your large-group facilitating team?
- How do you inform and invite people? How do you make sure that everybody who is needed is willing and able to attend the event?

Set the stage:

- Which venue?
- How many rooms of what size?
- What infrastructure do you need? Do you have the chairs, tables, podium, flip charts, white boards, corkboards, garbage bins, etc.?
- What technical equipment do you need? Do you have a projector, microphones, speaker, noise maker, computer, printer, etc.?
- What materials do you need for the work process? Do you have A4/A3 sheets, marker or pens, tape, sticky notes or index cards, cardboard, etc.?
- What does the seating order look like? How do you inform attendees of this order?

Accommodation, food, and drinks:

- Do people have to travel in order to participate? Do they need accommodation?

- If so, what coordination do you need? Do you want to provide travel or hotel information? Do you even want to organise this? Who covers the cost? What does the booking process look like?

- What does your large group need in terms of coffee/tea breaks, drinks, snacks, lunch, or dinner?

- Where will you provide all of this? Do you have to cater or does the hotel provide it?

Design the workflow:

- What does the kick-off look like? Who is hosting the event? Who does the official opening?

- What are the building blocks of the event? How do you activate people? Gather data? Generate insights? Decide what to do? Clarify how to follow up? Jointly close the event?

- Do you plan any outdoor activities or other forms of experiential learning to reenergise people and allow for different ways of exchange and learning?

Design the informal communication:

- Provide opportunity for informal gatherings in a self-organised way (open space in general, space around coffee machines, breakout rooms, etc.).

- Provide structure at lunch or dinner to allow for self-organised exchange.

- Decide if you want to plan a seating order to create even more differences or to leave it up to people to choose whom they meet and talk to.

- Decide if you want to have entertainment like music acts, a dance floor, magicians, and the like.

Design the collaboration process of the facilitators

- What are the key responsibilities of the facilitators? Why have them in charge?

- Who is doing what? Is there a lead facilitator? Are there any assistants?

- How do the facilitators stay in touch with each other during the event?
- How do the facilitators stay aligned with the sponsor(s)?
- Who does the documentation?
- How do they follow up with the event (retrospective, lessons learned, debriefing with sponsor, etc.)?

Figure 37: A large-group outdoor event.

World-café hosting guide

What is the world café about?

The world café helps to explore complex topics in a relaxed atmosphere. It is well known in the lean and agile space for its flexibility and the safe, almost informal environment it creates. Usually, there is a clear focus, a few questions, and the right people who gather around tables to answer these questions in a self-organised manner. Once again, an encouraging container is needed to make the most of it.

Why do we need the world café?

- It sets a clear focus.
- It brings the right people together.
- It provides clear boundaries for self-organised exchange.
- It creates a relaxed atmosphere for easy conversations on difficult topics.
- It encourages out-of-the-box-thinking and creative solutions.

How to make the most of it?

- Identify and invite the right people.
- Create a welcoming environment (natural light, music, plants, pictures, food, and refreshments).
- Provide a comfortable room and supplies:
    - small round or square tables that can seat four to seven;
    - a room large enough people to move comfortably among tables;
    - tables spread slightly chaotically, not in rows;
    - a piece of white flip-chart paper on top of each table;
    - a mug on each table filled with coloured markers; and
    - side tables for coffee, tea, water, or other drinks.
- Explain the purpose, the rules, and the logistics of the café:
    - X hosts for X subtopics sit at X tables (everybody else is a guest).
    - Each table has one host with a subtopic in line with the overall focus.

- Guests are free to choose the table that attracts them the most.

- There are three rounds of conversation, lasting 20-30 minutes each.

- Alternatively, you can trust the self-organising capabilities of the group and leave it to the guests to decide how long to stay at a table.

- Encourage everyone to contribute. Invite them to take notes, summarise key ideas, and draw on the table-top paper.

- Table hosts engage in the conversation as participants and stewards, not as formal facilitators. Usually, hosts share the essence of the conversation with guests who arrive for the next round.

- Harvest and share all ideas by presenting the "table recordings" and/ or have the hosts briefly report. What was the conversation like? What were the most important insights? What did they learn?

Open-space technology

What is the open space technology about?

Harrison Owen (1997) created a format for large group meetings that has become popular among lean and agile practitioners. It is based on four simple principles:

- Whoever comes are the right people.
- Whatever happens is the only thing that could have.
- Whenever it starts is the right time.
- When it's over, it's over.

Why do we need open space?

- It is a lightweight format for intense knowledge sharing.
- It creates an open yet encouraging container for intense exchange.
- It encourages self-responsibility and self-organisation on a broad level.
- It helps to discover fresh perspectives and innovative solutions.

How to facilitate an open space event?

The format can take from a few hours to two days. Here are some of its classic pillars:

- Participants are invited to gather in a circle.
- A host or lead facilitator introduces the format and its principles.
- Everybody is invited to sponsor topics they care about the most.
- Participants describe their topics on a sticky note and present them in turn.
- All topics are sorted in a so-called marketplace that provides a structure for where and when to meet to focus on any given topic.
- Topic owners host a session on their topic.
- Participants apply the "law of the two feet" to self-organise in the sessions of their choice, informally meet other participants, or take an individual break.
- Brief summaries of each session ensure information flow and sharing of knowledge.

Figure 38: An open-space gathering.

Lean coffee

//

What is the lean coffee about?

The lean coffee is a format for intensively discussing topics that participants care about. Since it is based on small time boxes, it encourages straight-to-the-point conversations and quick wins.

Why a lean coffee?

- It is an open format for exploring hot topics within a short period of time.
- It encourages everyone to participate.
- It is based on joint decision making.
- It can yield fresh impulses and innovative solutions with little effort.

How to facilitate a lean coffee?

Usually, it starts with a round of brainstorming during which everybody writes on sticky notes what is on his or her mind .

- All ideas are posted on a wall or on table, topics are clarified, duplicates removed, and similar items merged into one backlog.
- In order to decide which topics to talk about first, everyone is given two votes. This works best if everyone writes a dot on the notes of their two favourite topics.
- The topic that receives the most votes is placed in a "Discussing" column. The remaining topics are arranged in a "To Discuss" column based on popularity.
- Each topic is discussed for a set time, often five minutes. After that, people vote on continuing the discussion for another five minutes: a thumb up means "Yes"; "a thumb sideways is neutral; and a thumb down is "No".
- If the majority vote to continue, the group continues the discussion. If the majority votes not to, the facilitator puts that topic's sticky note into the Discussed column, and takes the next topic from the To Discuss column and places it in the Discussing column.
- The lean coffee ends when the group reaches the end of the predetermined time box (in most cases 45-60 minutes).

Often, I invite people to take a couple of minutes for debriefing, either in the form of a solo (a couple of minutes by yourself to review, digest, make notes) or in the form of a dialogue with a partner of your choice. If I use lean coffee as one of several building blocks within a training session or workshop, I also encourage people to briefly share their most important insights to facilitate both transparency and follow-up activities.

PART
EIGHT

Tools for changing

This section provides questionnaires, checklists, and guidelines for strengthening your changing capability. You can use these proven tools in various ways:

- to learn new things or remind yourself of things you may have forgotten;
- to map these things with your current practice;
- to create fresh ideas for your daily business;
- to run some experiments; and
- to put the wheels of learning into motion.

As argued in the chapter on changing, the tools should be applied with a systemic mind-set, i.e. with regard to the organisational context, the team, and your individual situation at hand. The section starts with a sample questionnaire for a personal retrospective. This kind of retrospective can be used as a springboard into learning and improvement. If you don't want to build only on your own ideas, you can ask for help by using tools such as feedback and feed-forward, the feedback planner, or the questionnaire for preparing tricky situations.

In order to foster change on a broader level, the format of a self-organising change team has proven to be helpful in many situations. Some guidelines may help you to effectively set up such a team. The following pages suggest tools any change team can make good use of. Stakeholder mapping can identify people affected by our change activities. A stakeholder interview can respectfully involve those who seem to be critical for the success of our efforts. A visual change-management system might support the completion of whatever initiative we start. I define the most important building blocks of such a system and provide some questions and tips that may guide you. Finally, two examples of change canvases will show how to create the pillars of any change effort you have in mind.

Personal retrospective questionnaire

//

This is a tool you can use on your own. Take some time from your job, best at somewhere you enjoy, and visualise whatever comes to your mind in regard to the core questions of your choice.

Here is a list of questions to select.

To focus on experiences:

- What am I currently happy with?
- What am I proud of?
- What worked well recently?
- What did I achieve?
- What was a highlight in my work?
- What did not work well?
- Where did I fail?

To focus on insights:

- What are the main reasons for my successes and failures?
- What skills and strengths can I build on?
- What are obvious weaknesses?
- Where do I see my biggest weakness and how does it hinder me?

To focus on decision-making:

- What conclusions can I draw from my experiences and insights?
- What should I improve on?
- Where would I like to focus?
- What action steps would I like to take?
- How can I ensure that I will take these steps?

Select the questions that resonate the most with you. You can either create a questionnaire on a sheet of paper or use sticky notes to record each answer. You can cluster and highlight these answers or simply distil your insights from a worksheet. I run a personal retrospective on a quarterly basis with no more than one improvement area, i.e. a few action steps to focus on between retrospectives. Each subsequent retrospective includes a review of my previous decisions and the action steps I've taken. Sometimes, I also crosscheck my decisions by asking for feedback before I start executing possible improvements (see next tools).

Exercises in looking into the future

Former CEO Charles Handy (2002) describes how to balance looking back and looking forward with these exercises. Read then, make your choice, and explore the fresh perspectives that can emerge from each of these exercises:

Exercise 1: Your lifeline

On a piece of paper, draw a line to represent your life from birth to death. Indicate with a cross where on that line you are now. Most people draw a line similar to the one below. Draw yours before you read on.

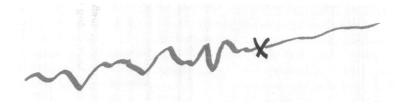

It is likely that you will draw a line with peaks and valleys. Explore what the ups and downs represent. These ups and downs will tell you something about your daily priorities and the position of your cross will tell you something about the proportion of your life ahead of you. Does the line aim upwards at the end or downwards? As Handy suggests, the answer will tell you something about your secret thoughts and hopes about the future.

Exercise 2: Your own obituary

Write your own obituary as if written by a good friend who knows you well and understands the "you" behind the facts. Don't write more than 200 words.

While it is a big challenge to imagine your own death as a real event, this allows you to think in more concrete terms about the time between now and your death.

The exercise forces you to stand at the end of your life and look backwards. In some way, it puts your current actions into a broader context and offers a fresh perspective. Share this with a real friend to learn more about what you will be remembered for.

Exercise 3: Your individual qualities

Imagine asking 10 friends to list one quality they like in you. List those qualities and identify two situations where each of those qualities has been useful in the past and one situation in which it could have been useful. This forces you to accentuate the positive in you and to conceive of other times your strengths and talents might be useful.

Feedback and feed-forward

Use this worksheet to prepare for peer feedback. Take time to review what you have experienced with the other worksheets, identify specific situations in your collaboration, and generate expectations for a better future. Usually, everyone on the team writes one worksheet for each of the others. Once all worksheets are finished, the team openly presents what is written on the sheets, best by having one team member at a time receiving all feedback, then taking turns. As described in the chapter on changing, I've had good experiences doing the exercise regularly to update the feedback, appreciate achievements and encourage further steps.

From: _____ To: _____

Date: _____

In order to improve our collaboration, I would like to ask you...

to maintain:

to do more of or more often do:

to do less of or cease:

and also:

The feedback planner

Paul Jerome provides easy guidelines for preparing as well as providing feedback in terms of four quadrants. Give it a try whenever you face a difficult situation with a team colleague or even your superior. Keep in mind that accurate feedback shows respect and helps each other to learn. As such, it is a key driver of change for any self-organising system.

NAME: **DATE:**

Describe current behaviours:	**Identify alternative behaviours:**
Describe what you want to reinforce (appreciate) or redirect (criticise) to improve a situation.	Agree on specific actions to improve the situation.
Be brief, descriptive, and specific.	Be encouraging, listen carefully, and achieve mutual understanding.
Check your dialogue partner's understanding and clarify open questions.	Feel free to provide your own ideas and offer further help, but not too early.
Identify situations:	**Describe impact and consequences:**
Describe specific situations where you observed these behaviours.	Ask your feedback partner about the effects of his or her current behaviour.
Be factual with examples.	Listen actively and check your own understanding.
Again, check for understanding and clarify questions.	Provide your own point of view, but not too early.

Tricky situations: Worksheet for preparation

//

This worksheet helps you to prepare to professionally handle tricky situations. Take time to review what you have experienced, gather relevant data, and generate insights to help you to come up with the right strategy. If in doubt, ask a friend, coach, or mentor for help so that you don't waste time and energy in pointless conversations.

What is the situation about? What does the context look like?

Who is involved? What's the background of the people involved?

What exactly do you want to achieve in your conversation?

How do you want to design and facilitate your conversation?

Guidelines for setting up a change team

//

As defined in the chapter on changing, a change team is a group of key players who are responsible for the successful implementation of organisational change. Whether or not you want to use a change team to manage the operational flow of your initiative(s) depends as much on the specific goals and contexts  as the question of who should be on the team. Here are, nevertheless, some guidelines on setting up a change team that have proven helpful for various senior managers:

1. **Clarify the necessity of a change team.** Does our initiative need a separate steering group? Do we need to align our initiative with other change efforts? Do we want to create a system for consistently managing all on-going initiatives?

2. **Define the mission of the change team.** What is the change team responsible for? What do we expect of them?

3. **Allocate people and resources.** Who is needed for the mission? Who should be on the team? How much time is needed? How do we make sure that all change-team members are available, i.e. can dedicate enough time and attention? What does the team need in terms of space, material, or external coaching?

4. **Set the boundaries for collaboration.** What about decision-making authorities? Is the change team free to make its own decision? What has to be aligned? What kind of feedback loops do you establish? How do you measure whether or not the change team fulfils its mission?

5. **Kick off change-team building.** What is needed to manage change with a sustainable pace? How do they organise themselves? What kind of ground rules and policies do they establish?

Stakeholder mapping

///

What is stakeholder mapping about?

We use the technique to make the power dynamics and involvement of your stakeholders visible. We identify possible conflicts and opportunities for cooperation, and translate needs into concrete action plans.

Why do we need it?

This exercise is particularly useful for:

- building a change team;
- kicking off a broader initiative;
- jointly creating awareness of the influence exerted by the relevant stakeholders;
- revealing fresh perspectives, which in turn can lead to new ideas for successful leadership and project management; and
- preventing conflicts by anticipating tensions and resistance.

How to make the most of it?

The aim of this intervention is to draw attention to the often-taboo subject of power structures. Although the analysis of relationship networks is always a delicate issue, it is nonetheless also very effective.

Provide a safe venue, set the right timeframe (60-90 minutes for a group of three to seven people), and have all the necessary equipment at hand (corkboard or whiteboard, index cards or sticky notes of different sizes, markers of different colours).

Follow the steps as described below.

Step 1

Together, the participants create a map of the relevant stakeholders and their influence on the project. In doing so, they consider the following factors:

KEY QUESTIONS	FACILITATOR'S ACTIONS
Who influences our success or failure?	Leading a call-out, listing individuals and groups
How strong is the respective influence?	Putting all relevant stakeholders on cards of different size
How close are the individual stakeholders to us and to each other?	Defining a centre (our mission or goal) and finding the right distances to this centre and to each other
What characterises the relationship between the different stakeholders?	Using symbols or different colours to visualise the quality of the relationships. You can even add "typical quotes" of each stakeholder.

Step 2

The participants use the stakeholder map to discuss the influence various stakeholders have on the project and their differing expectations for it. To generate more insights, you can start with more intimate dialogues by splitting up the group in pairs or trios. You can also invite the participants to put themselves in stakeholder roles and look at the project from these perspectives.

Step 3

The participants develop a specific strategy for each relevant stakeholder (group) that, in turn, leads to a concrete action plan (Who? What? When?).

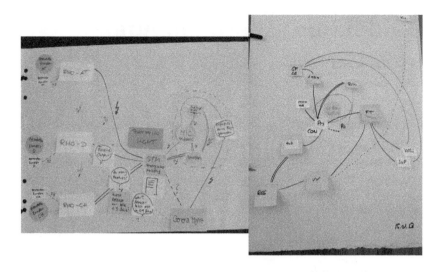

Figure 39: Examples of completed stakeholder maps.

Guidelines for stakeholder interviews

Once you have identified your most important stakeholders, how they presumably think about your change effort, and how they are connected which each other (see "Stakeholder mapping" on the previous pages), you should think about how to effectively involve them. Conducting interviews with stakeholders may help to answer this question. Here are some tips.

Preparing the interviews:

- Decide whom to interview and whether to do this in a one-on-one or team setup.

- Kindly ask the selected individuals or groups for some time to explore their points of view. Provide information about your change initiative if needed.

- Prepare for the interview.

Conducting the interviews:

- Set the stage in terms of expected outcome, process, and next steps.

- Conduct the interview by focusing on "What goes well in our process?" and "What should be improved?" If you work with larger groups, think of splitting them in pairs or trios to allow for more engagement and intimacy.

- Summarise their most important answers, best by inviting them to write their chosen top-three positive factors and challenges on index cards or sticky notes.

- Thank your interview partners for their time and willingness to openly share their points of view.

- Ask for open questions and clarify as much as needed.

- Remind them about the next steps.

Consolidating the interviews:

- Cluster the answers of your interview partners to see the big picture: "What can we build on?" and "What do we have to change?"

- Generate headlines for the most important positive as well as the most challenging clusters.
- Present these clusters/headlines to your stakeholders and ask for their feedback. Use this conversation as an opportunity to clarify how the envisioned change initiative helps to address the challenges.
- Achieve a consolidated list of expectations for your change initiative.

Visual change-management systems

Here are some guidelines for creating your own visual change-management system.

Start with what you do now by running a retrospective on former change initiatives:

- What worked well in the past?
- What did not work well?
- What have been the main reasons for your successes and failures?
- What conclusion can you draw from your insights?
- What would be needed to improve your change management?

Map your insights with what visual change management systems have to offer:

- How do your needs for improvement resonate with the practices of visualisation, limiting parallel activities, managing flow, and the like?
- How do you think that these practices can help to address your specific issues?
- What exactly do you want to achieve?
- How do you make a final decision on whether or not you want to establish a visual change-management system? Get a clear assignment from a sponsor.

Design your system for your specific context:

- What do the change items that are supposed to create value (epics, stories, activities) look like? Visualise typical items.
- What does the change process look like? Visualise the typical steps of your change stream.
- What is already in your system? Visualise all change items, put them in the right position in the system, and use avatars to clarify who is responsible for each item. Visualise any blockages.
- What do you have to agree on to effectively run your system? Agree on specific policies.

- How can you encourage flow? Think about setting change-in-progress limits in order to limit parallel activities.
- What feedback loops do you need to manage change flow? Define meetings, stakeholders, and metrics. Clarify whom to involve when and how often.

Kick off your system:

- How can you effectively run and continuously improve your system?

Change canvases

///

If you are keen to stick to small experiments rather than big change initiatives, I provide two similar tools that will get you started with an overview: the Lean Change Canvas designed by Jeff Anderson (2012) and the One-Page Change Plan/Strategic Change Canvas by Jason Little (2014).

TEAM / DEPARTMENT CHANGE CANVAS

TEAM VISION
WHERE DOES THE TEAM WANT TO BE IN 6 MONTHS? A YEAR?

WHAT IS SUPPORTING THE CHANGE?		WHAT IS WORKING AGAINST THE CHANGE?
	STRONG SUPPORT SEVERE BLOCK	

WHAT HELP DO WE NEED?
WHAT HELP DOES THE TEAM NEED TO CONTRIBUTE TO THIS VISION?

WHAT'S OUR PLAN	PREPARE	INTRODUCE	REVIEW
OPTIONS EXPERIMENTS WE CAN DO TO CONTRIBUTE TO THE OVERALL CHANGE STRATEGY COST / VALUE	EXPERIMENTS BEING PLANNED	EXPERIMENTS IN PROGRESS	EXPERIMENTS BEING REVIEWED AGAINST EXPECTED OUTCOMES

Lean Change Canvas
Brainstorm your organizational transformation

Urgency Top 3 drivers, and what needs to change	Target State Strategic pillars, common enablers, etc	Vision Single compelling statement that describes what the "destination" looks like	Communication 2 way path of communication	Change Recipients Who is impacted by the change
	Action Key methods used to impl change		Success Criteria Change will stick when:	
Capability of Org to Execute:		Key Behaviours:		Guiding Teams:
Required Investments Constraints around time, cost, and effort Commitment from recipients, leaders, and change agents		Wins Moral Performance Capability		

References

- Ackoff, Russell L. 1994. "From Mechanistic to Social Systemic Thinking". In Systems Thinking in Action Conference. Pegasus Communications. http://acasa.upenn.edu/socsysthnkg.pdf
- Anderson, David J. 2010. Kanban. Blue Hole Press.
- Anderson, Jeff. 2012. "Lean change part 2 - The lean change stack". Lean Transformation. http://agileconsulting.blogspot.ca/2012/08/lean-change-part-2-lean-change-stack.html
- Argyris, Chris. 1999. Organizational Traps. Oxford University Press.
- Beck, Kent, et al. 2001. "Manifesto for Agile Software Development" http://agilemanifesto.org/
- Burrows, Mike. 2014. Kanban from the Inside. Blue Hole Press
- Cohn, Mike. 2010. "The role of leaders on a self-organizing team". Succeeding with Agile. http://www.mountaingoatsoftware.com/blog/the-role-of-leaders-on-a-self-organizing-team/
- Cooperrider, David L, and Diana Whitney. 2005. Appreciative Inquiry: A Positive Revolution in Change. Berrett-Koehler Publishers.
- Crevani, Lucia, Monica Lindgren, and Johann Packendorf. 2010. "Leadership, not leaders: On the study of leadership as practices and interactions". Scandinavian Journal of Management 26: 77-86.
- "The Shift Index". 2013. Deloitte's Center for the Edge. http://www.deloitte.com/view/en_US/us/About/Catalyst-for-Innovation/Center-for-the-Edge/the-shift-index/index.htm
- DeMarco, Tom and Timothy Lister. 1999. Peopleware: Productive Projects and Teams. Dorset House. Second revised edition.
- Denning, Stephen. 2010. The Leader's Guide to Radical Management. Jossey-Bass.
- Derby, Esther. 2009. "When to stand back, when to step in", Esther Derby Associates, Inc. http://www.estherderby.com/2009/06/when-to-stand-back-when-to-step-in.html
- Derby, Esther, and Diana Larsen. 2006. Agile Retrospectives. Pragmatic Bookshelf.
- Doppler, Klaus, and Christoph Lauterburg. 2000. Managing Corporate Change. Springer.

- Dörner, Dietrich. 1996. The Logic of Failure. Metropolitan Books.
- Drucker, Peter F. 1999. Management Challenges for the 21st Century. Collins Business.
- Eoyang, Glenda H. 2002. Conditions for Self-Organizing in Human Systems. Ph.D. dissertation, Union Institute, Cincinnati, Ohio.
- Gardenswartz; Lee, and Anita Rowe. 2003. Diverse Teams at Work. Society for Human Resource Management.
- Gebert, Diether. 2004. Innovation durch Teamarbeit. Kohlhammer.
- Gonçalves, Luis, and Ben Linders. 2014. Getting Value out of Agile Retrospectives. InfoQ. http://www.infoq.com/minibooks/agile-retrospectives-value
- Hackman, J. Richard. 2002. Leading Teams. Harvard Business Review Press.
- Hamel, Gary. 2011. "First, Let ́s Fire All the Managers". In Harvard Business Review December 2011. https://hbr.org/2011/12/first-lets-fire-all-the-managers
- Hamel, Gary. 2012. What Matters Now? Jossey-Bass.
- Handy, Charles. 2002. The Age of Unreason. Random House Business.
- Heylighen, Francis. 2001. "The science of self-organization and adaptivity". The Encyclopedia of Life Support Systems 5 (3): 253-280 http://pespmc1.vub.ac.be/Papers/EOLSS-Self-Organiz.pdf
- Holman, Peggy, Tom Devane, and Steven Cady (eds.). 2006. The Change Handbook. Berrett-Koehler Publishers.
- Hope, Jeremy, Peter Bunce, and Franz Röösli. 2011. The Leader's Dilemma. Jossey-Bass.
- Hope, Jeremy, and Robin Fraser. 2003. Beyond Budgeting. Harvard Business Review Press.
- Hubbard, Douglas W. 2014. How to Measure Anything. Wiley. Third edition.
- Hundermark, Peter. 2014. Do Better Scrum. ScrumSense. Version 3. http://www.scrumsense.com/resources/do-better-scrum/
- Isaacs, William. 1999. Dialogue and the Art of Thinking Together. Crown Business.
- Jerome, Paul J. 1999. Coaching Through Effective Feedback. Pfeiffer.
- Kahneman, Daniel. 2011. Thinking, Fast and Slow. Farrar, Straus and Giroux.

- Kaltenecker, Siegfried. 2013. "Culture eats agile for breakfast". Platform for Agile Management. http://p-a-m.org/2013/09/culture-eats-agile-for-breakfast/

- Kaltenecker, Siegfried, and Bent Myllerup. 2011. "Agile and systemic coaching". Scrum Alliance. https://www.scrumalliance.org/community/articles/2011/may/agile-systemic-coaching

- Kaltenecker, Siegfried, and Mike Beyer. 2014. "Kanban on track – Evolutionary change management at the Swiss railways". InfoQ. http://www.infoq.com/articles/kanban-on-track

- Kaltenecker, Siegfried, Thomas Spielhofer, Sabine Eybl, Johanna Schober, and Stefan Jäger. 2011. Erfolgreiche Führung in der Agilen Welt. PAM. http://p-a-m.org/wp-content/uploads/2011/11/Erfolgreiche-Fuehrung-in-der-Agilen-Welt-Eine-Studie-der-PAM.pdf

- Katzenbach, Jon R., and Douglas K. Smith. 1992. The Wisdom of Teams. Harvard Business Review Press.

- Kegan, Robert, and Lisa Laskow Lahey. 2009. Immunity to Change. Harvard Business Review Press.

- Kerth, Norman. 2001. Project Retrospectives. Dorset House.

- Kniberg, Henrik. 2011. Lean from the Trenches. Pragmatic Bookshelf.

- Laloux, Frederic. 2014. Reinventing Organizations. Nelson Parker.

- Lencioni, Patrick. 2002. *The Five Dysfunctions of a Team*. Jossey-Bass.

- Leopold, Klaus. 2013. "Kanban and its flight levels". http://www.klausleopold.com/2013/07/kanban-and-its-flight-levels.html

- Leopold, Klaus and Siegfried Kaltenecker. 2015. Kanban Change Leadership. Wiley 2015.

- Liker, Jeffrey K., and Gary L. Convis. 2011. The Toyota Way to Lean Leadership. McGraw-Hill.

- Little, Jason. 2014. Lean Change Management. Happy Melly Express.

- Luhmann, Niklas. 1995. Social Systems. Stanford University Press.

- Manns, Mary Lynn, and Linda Rising. 2004. Fearless Change. Addison-Wesley Professional.

- Owen, Harrison. 1997. Open Space Technology. Berrett-Koehler Publishers. Second edition.

- Platform for Agile Management. http://p-a-m.org

- Parry, Charles, Mark Pires, and Heidi Sparkes Guber. 2006. "Action Review Cycle and the After Action Review Meeting". In The Change Handbook, edited by Peggy Holman, Tom Devane, and Steven Cady, 484-489. Berrett-Koehler Publishers.

- Poppendieck, Mary and Tom. 2010. Leading Lean Software Development. Addison-Wesley Professional.

- Raelin, Joseph A. 2003. Creating Leaderful Organizations. Berrett-Koehler Publishers.

- Reinertsen, Donald G. 2009. The Principles of Product Development Flow. Celeritas Publishing.

- Rother, Mike, 2009. Toyota Kata. McGraw-Hill.

- Rother, Mike, and John Shook. 2003. Learning to See. Lean Enterprise Institute. Version 1.3.Schaffer, Robert H., and Ronald N. Ashkenas. 2005. Rapid Results! Jossey-Bass.

- Schein, Edgar H. 2004. Organizational Culture and Leadership. Jossey-Bass.

- Schein, Edgar H. 2009a. Helping. Berrett-Koehler Publishers.

- Schein, Edgar H. 2009b. The Corporate Culture Survival Guide. Jossey-Bass. New and revised edition.

- Schein, Edgar H. 2013. Humble Inquiry. Berrett-Koehler Publishers.

- Schwaber, Ken. 2001. Agile Processes and Self-Organization. Control Chaos. http://www.controlchaos.com/storage/scrum-articles/selforg.pdf

- Schwaber, Ken, and Jeff Sutherland. 2013. The Scrum Guide. Scrum Guides. http://www.scrumguides.org/scrum-guide.html

- Seddon, John. 2008. Systems Thinking in the Public Sector. Triarchy Press Ltd.

- Simon, Fritz B. 2004. Gemeinsam sind wir blöd. Carl-Auer Verlag.

- Spear, Steven J. 2009. The High-Velocity Edge. McGraw-Hill.

- Sutherland, Jeff. 2008. "Self-Organization: The Secret Sauce for Improving Your Scrum Teams". YouTube video, 1:33:20. Posted by GoogleTechTalks, February 10, 2009. https://www.youtube.com/watch?v=M1q6b9JI2Wc

- The State of Scrum: Benchmarks and Guidelines. 2013. Scrum Alliance. https://www.scrumalliance.org/scrum/media/ScrumAllianceMedia/Files and PDFs/State of Scrum/2013-State-of-Scrum-Report_062713_final.pdf

- Weick, Karl E. 1995. Sensemaking in Organizations. Sage Publications.

- Weick, Karl E., and Kathleen M. Sutcliffe. 2001. Managing the Unexpected. Jossey-Bass.

- Weisbord, Marvin, and Sandra Janoff. 2007. Don't Just Do Something, Stand There! Berrett-Koehler Publishers.

- Wheatley, Margaret J. 2006. Leadership and the New Science. Berrett-Koehler Publishers.

- Yip, Jason. 2011. "It's not just standing up: Patterns for daily standup meetings" (2011), Martin Fowler. http://martinfowler.com/articles/itsNotJustStandingUp.html

About the author and acknowledgments

Siegfried Kaltenecker is the joint managing director of Loop Consultancy, specialising in organisation and leadership development and based in Vienna.

As an expert in Lean and Agile change management, Sigi has already been involved with multiple international companies such as Alcatel, bwin.party, eSailors, Kaba, ImmoScout24, Magna, RWE, Swiss Federal Railways, and Thales Group.

He is a certified systemic organisation consultant, ScrumMaster, Scrum Product Owner, and Kanban Coaching Professional. Sigi co-edits the Platform for Agile Management (p-a-m.org), has authored various articles on lean and agile topics and is co-author of Kanban Change Leadership, which will be published in English in 2015.

It is a truism that most complex artefacts cannot be accomplished without the help of others. They need feedback to grow and are co-created to some extent. This holds true for this booklet, too.

I want to thank Michael Beyer, Elisabeth Blum, Ana-Maria Ciobotaru, Louise Gardiner, Cliff Hazell, Klaus Leopold, Ben Linders, Jason Little, Lawrence Nyveen, Mike Rumpler, and Thomas Spielhofer for their valuable feedback and organisational support.

Special thanks to Peter Hundermark, who co-trained many leadership classes with me and helped to develop the topic. Moreover, he co-authored some parts of the introductory "Self-organising teams" chapter (as published on InfoQ).

My biggest thanks to Sabine Eybl for her long-term partnership in general and the many feedback loops throughout my writing process in particular.

www.ingramcontent.com/pod-product-compliance
Lightning Source LLC
Chambersburg PA
CBHW051234050326
40689CB00007B/921